Copyright

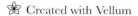

Cover Design: Dar Albert

Editing: **Michele Chiappetta** *of Three Point Author Services*

❋ Created with Vellum

ACKNOWLEDGMENTS

These things are so hard to write. It can't be as long as the book, but you fear leaving people out. So instead, I'll just go with the basics:

- To my father who gave me the gift of storytelling
- To Renee and Chris, without whom none of what I do would be possible
- To the Girls: Goody, Katy, Emma, Roz, Ava and Skylar
- To my Critical Reader and Focus Groups, JT Farrell and all of my readers – thank you from the bottom of my heart
- To Michele Chiappetta of Three Point Author Services, Editor Extraordinaire for all her hard work and putting up with my crazy schedule
- To Dar Albert of Wicked Smart Designs, the genius behind my covers who works with nothing

from me and produces the most amazing artwork, which then become my covers

SUBMISSION

MASTERS OF THE SAVOY

DELTA JAMES

CHAPTER 1

*M**ay 1, 1536***
Greenwich Palace
London, England

"My lady, the king loves you…"

"He does not. His fickle heart now belongs to Jane Seymour. The pasty-faced bitch can have him. I pray you do me this one last favor and watch over, as best you can, my daughter Elizabeth."

"But Queen Anne…"

"Have you not heard, Madge? I am no longer queen. Our marriage will be declared null and void—as if it never happened, and Elizabeth will be declared bastard."

"The trial..."

"…is nothing more than playacting so they can write it in the history books that I was tried and convicted. Henry seeks to turn his people on me, so he does not garner their disdain when he puts me aside as he did with Catherine. Know that I did not do what they accuse me of, but it will not matter. I will die so that Henry can have the Seymour spawn. She is not strong enough to carry his sons, and like Catherine, any he manages to get on her will die."

"My lady, do not say such things…"

"Why not? What more can they do? Kill me twice?" Anne paced back and forth. She had to ensure that Elizabeth would live. "Madge, please, one last favor?"

"Of course, my lady."

Anne pressed the small, intricately carved box, its edges sealed and then wrapped in cloth and dipped in wax, into Madge's hands. "Take this and make your way to Wolsey's wine cellar. In the very back, there is a small cask of malmsey wine that sits cradled in an elaborate holder. Beneath the back brace, there is a loose brick that conceals a hidden compartment. If you tip the cask forward, you can move the cradle, remove the brick and place the box inside, putting the brick back to seal the box within. Make sure no one sees you."

"Maybe you should try to run away?" suggested Madge, clearly frightened for her cousin.

"To where? I am the great whore of England, and the king wants me dead. So dead I shall be. Maybe I deserve it, not because I am guilty of that which I am accused, but because I coveted the husband of another woman for power… and yes, for love. I was a fool. Never surrender yourself to the notion of love, Madge. It does not exist. Now hurry. God bless you, Madge, and remember me in your prayers."

She watched her lady-in-waiting run to do her bidding one last time and then sat down to wait for the end to come. There had been a time she loved Henry and she thought he had loved her, but now she realized she had been nothing more than a pawn in a game of power in which she had no standing.

Anne sank to her knees and began to pray, not for her own soul, but for the Lord Jesus to watch over her daughter and keep her safe from the cruel machinations of men.

May 19, 1536
Tower of London
London, England

She was to die this morning. She had watched from the window of her cell as her brother, George, was beheaded just two days before. Her only remaining ladies in waiting beseeched her not to watch, but she felt responsible for George's death. He had done nothing but serve Henry faithfully and love her as a brother should. And now he was dead. In just a little while, she would join him. But if it were possible, she would find a way to cling to the realm that lay between this one and eternal joy.

They came for her—tall, burly men with weapons. What did they think she was going to do? Overpower them with her wit and fly away? Fools! But she could not condemn them for they only did their master's bidding. Master. The word made her want to retch. She had taken great care with her last appearance before the small crowd that had gathered to watch her die. She wore a dark grey gown of the finest material and an ermine mantle. She covered her hair with a white linen coif for purity.

Slowly she walked toward her execution, but not her final fate if she had anything to do with it. She paid the executioner and then turned to address the crowd in what would be recorded as her last words— at least in this time and place—her last only if she didn't find a way to hold on somewhere in the realm between Heaven and Hell.

"Good Christian people, I am come hither to die, for according to the law, and by the law I am judged to die, and therefore I will speak nothing against it. I am come hither to accuse no man, nor to speak anything of that, whereof I am accused and condemned to die, but I pray God save the king and send him long to reign over you, for a gentler nor a more merciful prince was there never: and to me he was ever a good, a gentle and sovereign lord. And if any person will meddle of my cause, I require them to judge the best. And thus I take my leave of the

world and of you all, and I heartily desire you all to pray for me."

Anne knelt, repeating the simple prayer, "O Lord, have mercy on me. To God, I commend my soul."

When the executioner called for his sword, she looked toward where it might come from. She felt pain only for the flash of a moment as the blade's clean, sharp edge removed her head from her body in a single blow. As her ladies wailed in grief, Anne felt free for the first time in her life. If there was a chance for another, she would take it—patience and planning would be her guides. The pull to go to the Light was strong, but she resisted, removing herself from its blinding path and returning to the dark tower.

One day, she vowed, *I will leave this place and live the life that was denied me. One day I will be free.*

Why was she not heading toward the Light? She had done nothing that would have sent her to the Dark or damned her soul. Had she been headstrong and proud? Yes. Had she not realized that while being a dominant personality was tolerable in a mistress, such behavior had to give way to a more submissive role as wife and queen to a tyrant? Most definitely yes, but she had been a good queen and could have been a great one.

The Warder of the Veil, as that was how he was

known, had watched from behind the Veil since the Tower had been built by William the Conqueror. He'd been witness to the murder of a mad and feeble king as well as the death of two children—young princes, and a threat to others' claim to the throne—but children, nonetheless. He'd seen it all, from the breathless high of a bride awaiting her wedding and coronation to the depths of despair upon the realization that there would be no clemency—in her case, only the mercy of a skilled swordsman instead of the ax.

Not much impressed or moved him anymore. He'd been cursed to walk between the two veils—one barring him from life and the other from the two possibilities that lay beyond: eternal joy or damnation. But she had surprised and impressed him. From the whispers he had heard, he had expected either an evil, heretical woman without a conscience or a scheming seductress. Anne had proved to be neither. She was a woman with strengths and shortcomings, like any other, but she had shown herself to be intelligent, poised and compassionate. Quite remarkably, she was far more prepared and resigned to her death than any who had gone before.

The Warder had waited for the executioner's blade to swing, removing her head from her body. As her soul lost its grip on the only life she had known, he'd stood by to reassure her and take her by the hand, leading her to the Light where her brother and others who had loved her waited. But

Anne had not turned toward the Light; she had turned away and begun to walk down the corridor back to the room where she had spent her final days…

He started after her, and found her standing at the window, gazing at the site of her own execution.

"I am here, Madam…"

"Majesty," she corrected, as she turned to look at him.

It struck him how composed she was—how unafraid.

He inclined his head. "Majesty. I am here to take you to the Light…"

"Then you have come in vain. I have no intention of going into the Light."

He was taken aback. No one refused to go to the Light. Those damned souls headed for eternal darkness often tried to escape their fate, but were dragged into the Dark by Azrael, the Archangel of Death. Azrael offered no comfort or reassurance to those who were damned; the Warder, on the other hand, was able to provide both to those in his charge.

"My Lady… Majesty," he quickly corrected when she arched her regal eyebrow at him. "You have no place here."

"I was murdered by a lecherous husband…"

"Which is only one of the reasons you are being accepted into the Light. The only other choice is the Dark, and you are not damned to that fate."

Her smile was practically beatific. "I have chosen another fate for myself."

The Warder was confused. "Majesty, there is no other choice."

"There is if I find another way. I will find my way back through the Veil and have a life of my own choosing. I will no longer be a pawn or subject to any man. I will have a life lived on my own terms."

"Majesty, there is no way back through the Veil."

"I will find one. I will wait and I will watch, but I will have my way."

She turned back toward the window.

 *ll Hallows Eve*
    Present Day
London, England

How could Felix have let him down?

Gabriel Watson, Head of Security for the Savoy Hotel, jogged up the stairs from the tube and headed toward the hotel. He'd been certain of the quartet of friends—Roark Samuels, Michael Holmes, Felix Spenser and himself—Felix would be the next to fall. The man he'd thought would be the perennial bachelor, Roark, had been the first when he had married the erotic romance writer, Sage Matthews. And then Holmes, a DSI with Scotland Yard, had become embroiled in a paranormal mystery and fallen for Rachel Moriarty. Watson had been sure it would be Felix who succumbed next. After all, he had female hotel guests throwing themselves at his feet on an almost daily basis.

He could hardly blame Holmes, or Roark for that matter. Both of his friends had found women who were so suited to them, it was almost as though they had been tailor-made for them. Watson had never found a woman that he could say the same thing about. There had been a few disastrous relationships when he'd been a U.S. Marine Raider, a special forces unit which utilized small, lethal teams to eliminate specific targets.

He'd been cashiered out of the Raiders when he'd been unfairly and wrongly accused of conduct unbecoming an officer. It wasn't that he hadn't had an affair with a superior officer's wife; it was that she had been a more than willing participant and had been separated from her husband at the time of their dalliance. The resulting general discharge made a career in law enforcement an unlikely path.

Gabe had found his way into hotel management in New York City. He'd decided to shake up his life and, on a whim, applied for the position as head of security for the venerated Savoy Hotel in London. Surprisingly, they'd hired him. It had proven to be an ideal match between man and institution. Gabe had fallen in love with London and had purchased his home in Soho—a roomy one bedroom flat that was easy to maintain—close to work and restaurants, pubs and shops.

Felix, the dignified Head Concierge at the Savoy, approached him as he entered the foyer of the grand hotel.

"Trouble?" Gabe asked.

"None that I'm aware of. However, I was wondering if I might talk to you at some point."

Gabe wrinkled his brow, confused. "What's going on, Felix? We're friends. You don't need an appointment to talk to me."

A shadow passed over his friend's face before he smiled and said, "As you know, it's Halloween. With everything that's going on in the world today, the hotel thought we would offer the children of our guests and all the employees a safe and festive way to celebrate the holiday. We've set up several of the meeting rooms and given guests who want to hand out candy special signs for their doors. We're hoping we could get some of your people up on the floors and in each of the public rooms."

"Kind of short notice, but I'm sure some of my people will be up for it."

"Yes. Sorry about that. We've been planning it, and just this morning it occurred to us that it might be nice to have some additional security, just in case."

"I agree wholeheartedly. If you hadn't thought to ask, I would have been pissed, so we're good. Anything else before I get my day started?"

"Not that I can think of."

"Then I'd best get on it. I'll talk to you later."

Gabe headed into his office and was soon lost in various messages, meetings and planning sessions to get ready for the evening and then looking forward to several upcoming events.

Saoirse Madigan consulted the runes again. There was no denying what she'd seen over the past week—something was coming. She didn't know who, what or why, but she did know where: *London*. She cast around her farmhouse looking for her mobile. She knew that many people were never without the bloody things in their hands, but Saoirse often misplaced hers and resisted having what amounted to an electronic leash.

She'd spent the last two nights out at the standing stones and couldn't feel any kind of disruption. Last night, however, she'd cast her senses toward London, where she had a small group of people who had become good friends and had felt a slight disturbance. She cast the runes again and confirmed there was something, not necessarily evil, but something and it was in London.

Glancing at the phone, she realized how early it was. Saoirse had set up her business so that her time was her own. She accepted orders for the compounds she made, and it was easy for people to visit her website and enter their information. Once she confirmed everything with their prescriber, the person making the order submitted payment, and Saoirse then made and shipped the resulting potions and remedies. It gave her the freedom to choose her own schedule, and she planned to take advantage of it now.

She got dressed and threw together a bag of clothes. If she hurried, she could just make the ferry and be in London this afternoon. She'd call her friend Rachel Moriarty en route. Within half an hour, she was on her way.

"Saoirse," Rachel greeted her when she picked up the call. "How are you? Is everything okay? I don't normally hear from you on All Hallows Eve."

"Aye, I know. But I'm headed into London."

She looked outside. The weather itself was mild enough for the end of October, although the sky seemed off—neither bright nor dreary. The sun was out, but seemed to be playing peek-a-boo, using the wispy clouds as cover.

"Are you all right?"

Saoirse laughed. "I just have a bit of business I need to do that is most easily done in London. Do you know if the Savoy has any vacancies?"

Rachel was a dear friend and one of the kindest people she'd ever known. Her relationship with DSI Michael Holmes had only been a surprise until she'd seen them together. They had defeated one of the great evils of all time, and it had strengthened both of them and forged a powerful bond between them. Saoirse hated to be less than forthcoming with her friend, but she didn't know enough about what she was feeling to share it with anyone.

Besides, she really did have a few errands that would be done more easily in England's capital, and one that could only be done there.

"I don't know, but I can find out. We'll make it work. There's going to be a kind of progressive, moving party for the kids of the guests and employees, but before it gets going, we were going to have dinner with the gang. Please say you'll join us?"

"I'd love to. What time?"

"About six. Call me before you get to the hotel. We have yet to figure out where it is we're eating."

"Good. I'll see you then. And Rachel, will Felix be there?"

"Yes. The very dishy Head Concierge will be with us. Anything there I should know about?"

"Quit! Just because you found some lovely, dominant hunk who sees to all your needs doesn't mean the rest of us get to be so lucky."

"For what it's worth, he asks about you too. I'm just saying it might not be the worst thing in the world…"

"And what would the head concierge of the Savoy Hotel be doing on a farm on the coast of Ireland?"

"Maybe looking after all your needs, when he isn't

needed here. The two of you could split your time between the farm and London."

"Gawd, Rachel, but you're an incurable romantic."

"My expertise is in an era where romance had a great deal of power."

"Men ruled with the power of money and the sword."

This was an old argument between them.

"Aye," said Rachel, mimicking Saoirse's brogue, "and women befuddled them with their sensuality and intelligence."

"I know you're a big fan of the doomed queen, but if Anne Boleyn was so smart, how'd she end up with her head cut off?"

"Because Henry VIII was a misogynistic monster. I always wonder if she would have found happiness if she'd lived in another time or another place. She really was quite remarkable, and she changed the fate of England forever. Not only did she jump-start the Reformation, but she gave England one of its greatest monarchs."

"But she lived in the time and place she did and ended up with her head on the block because fat old King Henry wanted to fuck a more malleable, younger woman, so he disposed of Anne. She didn't even rail at the bastard on the scaffold."

"No. She knew she would die and chose instead to try and placate Henry in order to keep her daughter, and others who had been her supporters, safe."

"You really do like her…"

"Honestly? She's my favorite woman in history. I just think there is so much we don't know, and a lot of what we do know is suspect. History is always written by the victors."

Rachel promised Saoirse she'd arrange a place for her to stay, and reminded her to meet them at the Savoy. Saoirse drove to the ferry, enjoyed the ferry ride itself and then made her way into London. She figured her first stop would be Ye Olde Coin Shoppe, located close to the Tower of London. Knowing that finding a parking space at this time of day in the bustling area would be difficult, if not impossible, Saoirse chose instead to drive first to the Savoy Hotel on the Strand. Traffic in London was notorious no matter the time of day and parking even worse. Saoirse was often surprised people weren't murdered for a premium spot, but then Londoners normally prided themselves on being civil.

"Ms. Madigan, welcome back to the Savoy," said one of the valets. "Your room is ready for you. Would you like us to take your bags up?"

"Yes, and could I have a driver drop me close to the Tower?"

"Absolutely. If you'll just go sign in, we can take care of the rest."

Saoirse entered the beautiful lobby, smiling. The

Savoy's service was second to none. Staying here was more expensive than most of the other hotels in London, but she wasn't going to be here but a few days, and they made things so easy.

"Saoirse, welcome back to the Savoy," said Felix, coming forward to greet her.

It was hard to believe such an attractive man was the concierge at the hotel. Not that there was anything wrong with good, honest work, but Saoirse didn't think that Sage Matthews, the bestselling romance writer, had pictured him this way—tall, sleek, lean, like a powerfully built, predatory cat. He had a small, vertical scar by his left eye, which didn't mar the perfection of his face, but rather sharpened it and gave it character. He had deep brown eyes, a sensual mouth, and chestnut brown hair that was always meticulously styled.

"Felix. It's nice to see you again. Rachel says we're having dinner tonight."

"Yes, we're going to have it up in Roark and Sage's room as Gabe and I need to remain in the hotel for the trick-or-treat festivities."

"Good, I'll see you at six."

She left the foyer, happy to know she would get to see Felix later. She didn't understand her attraction to him. Gabriel Watson was usually more her type. Watson, Holmes and Moriarty—sometimes the universe had a real sense of humor. But something

about Felix's lean, muscular elegance made the butter-
flies in her belly take flight.

After being helped into the vintage touring car,
she gave the driver the address to Ye Olde Coin
Shoppe, which was located close to the Tower of
London.

"Any idea how long you'll be?" he asked.

"At least half an hour, I'd say, but if that interferes
with your schedule, I can either take the tube back,
catch a cab or just wander around until an appointed
time."

"Could you wander for, say, ninety minutes? If so,
I can go back to the Savoy and take another guest to
an appointment they have."

"Absolutely, but if I spend more than the hundred
pounds I'd planned to, I'm blaming it on you."

The driver laughed. "Sounds about right to me.
Thank you." He stopped in front of the shop, letting
her out, tipping his cap and returning to the driver's
seat.

She entered the shop—it was one of her favorite
places. Saoirse had known the owner for some time.
And if he knew you, there were all kinds of things
that could be purchased when the price was right.
Saoirse had been on the hunt for a mortar and pestle
from the Tudor era—specifically one that had been
used at Hever Castle, supposedly to cure Anne Boleyn
of the sweating sickness.

Saoirse loved shops like this one—they weren't

well lit, they were messy, the aisles were often not quite side enough to slip through easily. And yet they invited you to linger and to search through everything. One always felt like there was some treasure to be unearthed, some hidden prize amidst all the junk. Saoirse was a sucker for places like this. Even knowing what she knew about them, she couldn't stay away and often spent far more time sifting through the items on display than she should.

"But Miss, you must have some kind of provenance for the coins or identification," said Arthur Pole, the shop's owner. "You know, proof of who you are, where the coins came from—something that proves you and the coins are who and what you say you and they are."

"I told you," said a cultured female voice, "my purse with all of my papers has been stolen, and I need to exchange these coins. Are you telling me they are worth nothing?"

"No. In fact, they are quite valuable. You must understand that if these were found to be stolen…"

The woman, who from behind looked to be a few years younger than Saoirse, straightened her back, her bearing becoming regal. "Are you calling me a thief, sir?"

"Arthur? Might I be of assistance?" asked Saoirse as she approached.

The woman turned to face her. She was not beautiful in the conventional sense. She was taller than average, with an almost perfectly oval face and black hair. She had a lovely, trim figure and there was an air of grace and composure about her. Her eyes were dark brown and she looked somewhat familiar, but Saoirse couldn't quite place her.

CHAPTER 3

*a*nne took a deep breath and smiled. She must not panic. There was no way they could know who she was, where she had come from, or most importantly, when. She and the Warder of the Veil had struck up a friendship of sorts over the past five hundred years. Only twice each year did they come into conflict—May 19th and October 31st—the anniversary of her execution and All Hallows Eve. The latter, of course, was the time when the Veil between the two planes of existence was at its thinnest and provided her with the greatest chance of escape.

She had long ago decided to try and permeate the Veil to slip from the Void between the two worlds back into that of the living. Although the Warder had no desire to see her go into eternal darkness, he was honor bound not to allow her to return to the land of the living.

"It is not natural, my lady," the Warder intoned.

After the first three hundred years, Anne had relented and allowed him to address her by the more familiar term of my lady versus Majesty or Queen Anne. As she had pointed out, she had paid for those titles with her head, and she was damn well entitled to them.

"Having one's head cut off is not natural either. I was denied a life. My daughter, whom Henry despised and vilified me for, was one of England's greatest monarchs. I am entitled to the life that was taken from me—first by my father, then by my uncle and last by the king."

"One does not simply re-enter the land of the living..."

"Why not? Why am I once again subject to laws I had no voice in making? You have seen the time pass, as have I. Women are no longer the chattel of men. We are not yet their equals, but we have come so far. I watch from my window and from these halls, and I can see where I could make a life for myself. Not a big or fancy life, but a life where I could live again."

"There is no way back, My Lady."

"There is. You and I have both heard tales that on All Hallows Eve or the night before one's violent death, the Veil can be broken through if one has the heart and the stomach for it. I assure you I have both."

"And if you falter, Azrael will collect your soul and carry you into eternal torment and darkness. Are you willing to risk that?"

She turned and regarded him coolly. "Yes. A thousand times, yes. I have languished here for centuries. This is my time. I can feel it."

"I cannot allow it."

"And I cannot allow you to stop me."

As the great clock they called Big Ben struck three in the morning, when the mists and fogs of the City of London filtered through the open windows and swirled gently around and inside the Tower, Anne had slipped away from her watch dog. She knew that she must get through the Veil today—All Hallows Eve. She had felt the cold fingers of Azrael grasping for her several times over the past century—the other side wanted her to leave the Void. And so, she would… just not in the way it wanted her to.

Azrael wailed as he sailed through the hallways, not bound by mortal obstacles such as walls. Anne ran toward the door through which she had last walked as a mortal. Normally, she could not pass beyond any of the portals of the tower, but she believed her escape would be found through that one doorway. She ran down the steps, feeling Azrael closing in behind her, his wailing growing louder, almost deafening her as he closed in.

Anne knew if she could not penetrate the Veil that separated the Void from the land of the living, she would be trapped, and Azrael would have his prize— her soul. She would be damned to an eternity of torment and sorrow. But he would not catch her. She would escape. She would return. As the gnarled and cold hand of the Angel of Death reached for her, grasping the tendrils of her dark, silky locks, she put on a last burst of speed and propelled herself through the doorway that had led to Tower Green, the site of her execution.

She hit the barrier just as Azrael tried to close his fist around her hair. He shrieked in triumph, but Anne snatched her hair from his grasp and catapulted herself through the barrier. She tumbled onto the ground, hitting her shoulder and then her hip as she rolled away from the tower and onto the green grass.

No one was there to see her on this side of the barrier. Azrael screamed in frustration and anger at the doorway. She looked up to see the Warder of the Veil at her window. She rose to her feet and raised her hand in a sad sort of farewell, before turning toward the living quarters of the Yeoman Warders of the Tower.

Anne had watched over the centuries and knew where they were located, but more importantly, where she could find modern clothing. She reached the laundry facility. Making sure no one was there, she quietly entered and looked through clean clothes as her famous gray dress, worn at her execution, and all her undergarments began to fade away. She smiled as the sound of small gems and coins she had sewn into the hems and cuffs of her dresses hit the floor. She had wanted to ensure that if somehow she escaped her execution or found a way back, she would have money. She made a purse of sorts out of a square of fine linen weave and placed all her valuables inside, tying the four corners together.

The dress's disintegration might have left her naked, but it had also left her with enough wealth to see her through these first few days. If Madge had been true, then she might still have a fortune waiting for her in Wolsey's wine cellar—if it even still existed.

Pawing through clean clothing, she was able to assemble an outfit she thought might not look too out of place and then went in search of some kind of shoes or boots and a coat to ward off the night chill. She was in luck, because she found both after a very short search. Now, to find a place to hide until the gates opened and she could slip away.

Anne had spent her time in the Void learning— listening to people and watching as the passage of time had unfolded before her. She would need identification, and for that she would need modern currency. Two coin merchants had wandered through the tower one afternoon and she had followed them, listening and learning. She made note of Arthur Pole's shop. Surely he was related to Maggie Pole, the Kingmaker's granddaughter, who had been tried and executed for treason and had made her way from the block to eternal joy without so much as a wrong step.

But not Anne. No, Anne had made it back to the land of the living, and she meant to make the most of it.

She found a hidden niche among the gardens and,

pulling the great cloak around her she curled into a ball, concealing herself among the bushes. There, she slept until the sound of people and the sun's warmth had awakened her.

As those who prepared the Tower for its daily influx of visitors entered the fortress, Anne slipped away and out into the morning rush of London's busy day. She'd found some current money tucked inside the coat she had purloined. Transferring it to a deep outer pocket, she had stashed her coins and jewels in the concealed pocket where she'd found the folded paper currency.

When she passed by a street vendor, the delicious aroma of steamed meat pies was more than she could resist. Buying one and a container of water, she had wandered off, losing herself in the crowd and finding a bench to sit on. She watched as others twisted the top of their containers to get to the liquid. Doing the same, she took her first drink of cold, clean water. It was delicious. No wine, ale or mead had ever tasted as good or been as soothing to her parched throat.

She had worried that she might suddenly age and disintegrate as her clothing had done, but so far so good. Her skin, what she could see of it, remained soft, supple and without blemish, except for the scar where the executioner's blade had first struck. She overheard two women talking about a toilet facility, and she knew from listening and wandering the tower that this was where one performed one's morning ablutions.

Anne smiled and breathed a sigh of relief as she saw the privacy stalls. She took the largest one at the end, and after she was through, wondered what to do with the soiled paper. She was going to add it to the small can that seemed to contain some of the same when she heard a whooshing sound. She turned to see the water in the bowl, whirling around and then going down a funnel of some sort.

She dropped the paper in the now clean water, sat down and when she stood back up, it flushed again. *Ah,* she thought, amused at the cleverness of it. There must be a water sewage system of some sort that ran beneath the building marked 'toilet.'

She left the stall and followed the example of the other women, turning on running water, washing her hands, drying them off and then throwing the paper away. What a marvelous society this was, to have enough paper to discard it when it had been used. In her times, paper was an extreme luxury. She made her way on foot, marveling at being so close to all the things she had only glimpsed from the tower.

Knowing she would one day escape, Anne had spent her time watching, listening and learning. She knew she would have to be careful in order to keep from being discovered or at least questioned by the authorities. There had been forgers in her day. Surely there were some now, but they would cost money. And so, she made her way to Arthur Pole's place of business—Ye Olde Coin Shoppe.

The woman facing her looked so familiar. Saoirse wondered if it was one of those instances where the woman was out of place—that had they been somewhere else, she would have recognized her immediately.

"Saoirse," said Arthur Pole. "I have the mortar and pestle you wanted. The provenance is impeccable. I can't seem to make this lady understand I can't just take her coins…"

"He thinks me a thief or some kind of forger," the woman said in impeccable English.

"I didn't say that," said Arthur pleadingly.

"Either you believe me and will exchange these few coins, or you do not and are unwilling to help me. I wonder what the authorities would think of the agreement you made with your friend?"

"What friend?" Pole said, looking around nervously.

"The one with the Germanic accent whom you met with a fortnight ago at the Tower…"

Saoirse arched her eyebrow at Pole. "Arthur, it sounds to me like you're up to your old tricks. The Yard won't like hearing that."

"Now, see here, Saoirse. There's no need for

that…"

The woman smiled at her—her eyes alight with amusement—before turning back to the proprietor. "I am so glad to hear that. Now, what will you offer?"

"Be fair, Arthur. I don't have your expertise, but I'll know if you're trying to cheat her."

"She doesn't have identification with her," said Arthur, belligerently.

"Arthur, you and I both know you've done plenty of transactions off the books. I tell you what, if you quit giving my new friend here—" Saoirse turned to the woman questioningly.

"Anne. Anne Hastings."

"If you just pay Anne what the coin is worth, I'll buy my mortar and pestle and we'll be on our way."

Saoirse extended her hand. The woman looked down at Saoirse's hand as if confused by the implied invitation to shake it. Tentatively the woman took Saoirse's hand, and Saoirse closed her fingers around the woman's hand and gave it a gentle shake.

"Saoirse Madigan. Would you like to get a cup of tea and maybe a scone? There's a great little place right around the corner."

The woman smiled, a genuine smile not meant to beguile or seduce. "I would love to."

Arthur concluded his business with both women, grumbling the entire time.

As they left the shop, Saoirse said, "Don't mind Arthur. He's not a bad sort…"

"No. He is just a man who seems to think he can take advantage of women. It is disheartening to see how little some things have changed."

They made their way to a coffeehouse not far from Ye Olde Coin Shoppe. Saoirse found them a somewhat isolated spot in the back and ordered for them both.

"I am not trying to be rude, but you stare at me as if we are old friends."

Saoirse nodded. "I don't mean to stare, my lady. You should know I am a witch, but I mean you no harm."

"That is not a term I would cast about in a public place, and what makes you think I am of the nobility?"

Saoirse leaned in closer, lowering her voice so as to not be overheard easily. "Not nobility. Royalty. I don't suppose you would be comfortable calling yourself or anyone else a witch, but I wanted to put that on the table and tell you this: I don't know what you're doing here, but I will help you in any way I can."

"You act as if you know me."

"Obviously, I don't know you. But I know who you are, or were, once before. There are few who wouldn't notice your likeness, but only those of us who can feel the disruption in the planes of existence would know your true identity… Queen Anne Boleyn."

CHAPTER 4

*A*nne glanced around quickly and then regarded the woman across the table from her. *How does she know who I am? Is she truly a witch? Does she mean to try and send me back? I won't go.*

"That is preposterous," she declared. "Queen Anne has been dead for centuries. She was beheaded on Tower Green. Does my head appear to be missing?" Her tone was light-hearted, as if she were making a joke.

"I swear to you," the witch said. "I mean you no harm and will help in any way I can."

The woman looked and sounded sincere, but Anne knew better than to accept those words at face value. After all, it had been her own sister-in-law who had offered the most damning evidence against both her and her brother, George. Few women in Anne's life had been people she could trust… and even fewer men.

Anne gave a little laugh. "Ah, so we are playing a game. If I were truly Queen Anne and you were a witch, what possible help could you give me?"

The witch, Saoirse she called herself, smiled. "I already assisted you with Arthur at the coin shop. I have to tell you, trying to redeem the coins you have for today's currency is going to be difficult without proper identification. I know those who can help you with that. I'm going to guess you came through the Veil sometime earlier today. You'll need a place to stay and get acclimated to our time. I can help with that as well."

She wanted desperately to believe that Saoirse desired to help. It would make adjusting to her new life so much easier. "Why should I trust you?"

"That's a good question—to which I can only answer, because I want to help. And if you'll let me, I have a small group of friends who would help as well…"

"No. No one else can know. I broke free, but I am not sure they won't be looking for me."

Saoirse's eyes sparkled. "All the more reason to let me help you."

"Why?"

"Because I'm a witch. Because you have fascinated people for centuries. Because you found a way back from the other side. Because, well, why not?"

For the first time since her mad escape, Anne smiled with true happiness—it looked as though she had found an ally. "What would you suggest?" she asked.

"You'll need documentation, but we can get by without it for a day if you'd rather rest. I have a hotel room—lodgings—and you are more than welcome to stay with me. It isn't Hever Castle or Greenwich Palace, but it's lovely and the staff is accommodating. We can talk without fear of being overheard."

"I am not given to trusting, but I do not believe I have much choice."

"I swear to you, I only want to help."

Anne nodded. "Very well."

"If you're finished with your tea, let's get to the hotel. I have hired transportation coming."

"One of those wheeled vehicles that have no horses?"

"Yes, we call them cars. They are incredibly safe."

Saoirse paid the bill, and they left the little shop and went back to stand in front of the coin merchant. A large car, as Saoirse had named it, pulled up; the coachman got out and helped them into it. Intrigued, Anne brushed her fingers over the butter-soft leather and leaned down to touch the soft carpeting underfoot. The glass in the windows was so clean and clear, and the whole coach had a wonderful, fresh scent that contained the faintest trace of citrus.

It was hard to keep from gawking at all of the

marvelous sights. They followed a wide road along the Thames—she would recognize that landmark anywhere—until they pulled up in front of an enormous and elegant building. The car stopped, and two individuals whom she thought must pass as footmen in this age opened the doors and helped them both out.

Saoirse led them into an enormous foyer where people were milling around. The witch waved to people behind some sort of large desk area and led her into a smaller foyer with a number of doors, several of which opened to allow those inside to exit and others to enter. Saoirse held her back until at last a set of doors opened to allow people to escape, so that she and Saoirse had the compartment to themselves. The doors closed of their own volition, and Anne reached out to touch the smooth exterior, intrigued yet again by this new world she found herself in.

Then, she felt the compartment move. Off balance, she looked for something to hang onto.

"It's all right, my lady. The elevator allows us to go up in the building without using the stairs," Saoirse assured her..

"Truly?" Anne asked, fascinated. "Is this your magick?"

"No. It's all done electronically. Please don't ask me to explain all of it, as I really don't know how it works."

Anne relaxed. "But we are safe?"

"Yes. No safer place in London."

The box they stood in ceased to move, and the doors opened again with a soft whoosh. Saoirse placed her hand under Anne's elbow, steered her off the contraption, and guided her down the hall. They stopped in front of a door, and Saoirse pushed several buttons on a small box attached to it, causing red and green lights to flash. The motions produced a soft, audible click before Saoirse opened the door. They stepped into a small foyer and from there a lovely sitting room with objects the purpose of which Anne could only guess at, and an enormous window with a balcony overlooking the Thames.

"I know this is modest compared to what you're used to…" started Saoirse.

"The room is lovely, and you are most kind to offer your assistance. As much as I fear your power as a witch, it must concern you that I have risen from the dead, so to speak."

"Not as much as it would someone who isn't used to things out of the ordinary revealing themselves. Are you tired? Hungry? Thirsty? Would you like a bath?"

Anne sighed. "Would it not be too much trouble to bring hot water from the kitchens?"

Saoirse laughed. "Let me introduce you to the modern bath."

She led Anne into a smaller room, where Anne

was delighted to see it had some of the fixtures she'd seen in the ladies room earlier in the day.

"Some of these things I recognize from when I first escaped. The toilet, the sink with running water…"

"Do you know it has running hot water?" asked Saoirse.

"No," Anne gasped. "How marvelous! So, we can fill the tub?"

"The tub has its own faucet with hot and cold water so it's easy to fill it, and the Savoy provides robes for its guests," Saoirse said, showing them to her. "But I think you might love the shower—hot and cold water that comes from up here like a rainfall."

"No, really?"

"Yes. There's soap and shampoo for washing and conditioner for softening your hair. If you want to take a tub bath…"

"No, I think I would like to try the shower," she said, over-enunciating the last word, testing it out.

"Okay, let me get it running and show you how to adjust the temperature of the water. And here's the best part—it will stay at that temperature."

Anne laughed. "What a marvelous innovation."

Saoirse got the shower running, adjusted the temperature and showed Anne how to do it.

"I'll leave you to enjoy it," said Saoirse, "but I'll be right out here if you need anything. I don't know about you, but I'm hungry. How about if I order some lunch? They'll bring it to us."

"Yes, thank you, Saoirse."

The door closed and Anne quickly disrobed, hanging her things on the hooks provided. Stepping into the shower and closing the glass door, she moaned in delight as the warm water fell on her skin, lightly peppering it like a good rain. She just stood under the water for the longest time, letting it revive her. Soon, she found the shampoo—what a curious name!—and washed her hair, reveling in the rich, luxurious suds that covered her head. Anne rinsed them out and then applied conditioner.

As this was the first time she'd ever conditioned her hair, she let it sit while she took the washcloth—at least, that item was the same after all these years; only this one was much softer—then lathered it up with soap and began to wash herself. It was such a gentle feeling to tend to herself this way, but still… Between the water pelting down on her skin, the aroma of soap, the shampoo and the conditioner, her skin came alive, and she realized how much she had missed the feeling of a man's hands running over her body.

For the last ten years of her life, it had only been Henry's hands that caressed her. She closed her eyes, imagining the way he used to cup her breasts before rolling her nipples between his thumb and forefinger, often giving them a little pinch before taking one and then the other into his mouth. She slid the cloth down the front of her body and between her legs. As it passed over her love pearl, the feelings it evoked made her legs shake. The 'little death' wasn't far off.

She snatched her hand away. It had been frowned upon for ladies to pleasure themselves, and Henry had forbidden anyone to touch her sexually in the ten years they were together—seven before he married her and then the three they were married. She wondered how history had recorded that. Had they deemed her inability to give him a son as her failure? Had they known about the impotency? The times he rolled off her, leaving them both frustrated and unfulfilled. How was she to give him a son or even get pregnant if he was unable to deliver his seed to her womb?

Sighing, she rinsed the cloth and then herself, leaving the final rinse to remove the conditioner from her hair to the last. She stepped out and grabbed a warm, fluffy towel. Running it over her skin, she moaned. Sheer heaven.

There came a light tap on the door. "My lady, lunch should be here any time and I have a comb if you'd like to join me."

Anne slipped into the robe and opened the door. "That was the most amazing experience. Does everyone have one of those?"

"A shower? Yes. Most people who have shelter of some kind, at least." She held up a large comb with wide teeth. "I can help you comb your hair out."

"No. I am no longer Queen, and I doubt I shall

have servants. You should call me Anne, and I will try not to be a burden."

"I spoke with my friend, Rachel. We have known each other a long time. She can and will keep your secret if you choose to share it with her. She's a history professor, specializing in the War of the Roses up through your daughter's reign. You and Elizabeth are particular passions for her."

"You would trust this woman with knowledge that you are a witch?"

"It's not as big a deal as it was in your time, but I would trust her with my life. Shall I call her?" Saoirse raised a small box in her hand.

"On one of those devices?" Anne wondered, pointing to what the other woman held.

Saoirse nodded. "Yes. It's called a mobile phone or mobile."

As Saoirse made her call, Anne began to run the comb through her hair. She had often hated washing her hair, as it snarled so easily and it was often difficult or painful to untangle it, but the wide teeth of the comb just seemed to slip through without any trouble. Anne walked to the balcony and attempted to open the heavy glass door, but it was either stuck or locked.

"Anne, allow me. Rachel is on her way over. I just told her I needed to meet with her before we went to dinner with friends."

"A good friend if she required no other explanation."

"That she is. This is the lock for the door."

Saoirse unlocked and opened it, allowing the chilled air to rush over Anne's body. It had been so long since she'd felt anything. The Void did not allow for much sensory input. She could see and hear things, but the other senses were lost, even touch. She could feel an object was solid, but couldn't truly feel its texture, temperature or much else about it. Now, all her senses were filled with so much information that it almost overwhelmed her.

"Your friend lives here?"

"No, but fairly close by car. She and her husband were going to meet here with our other friends for dinner. But if you don't feel up to a gregarious gang, you can stay here, or I can feign not feeling well and stay with you."

Anne smiled. "You are far too kind to me, Saoirse. I appreciate everything you have done thus far."

"It is my pleasure. I didn't know what you might like so I ordered way too much—soup, a couple of different sandwiches and shepherd's pie. I also ordered crème brûlée and tiramisu for dessert."

The knock on the door to the hall startled Anne, and she jumped.

Saoirse smiled in reassurance. "It's just room service. I doubt anything looking for you would be so polite."

Anne laughed. "I fear you are right. I have no proof that anyone is looking for me, but the Warder of the Tower had always said there is no escape. And Azrael…"

"Who are they—this Warder and Azrael?"

"Azrael is the Angel of Death, and the Warder is the one who leads those who die at the Tower, and are not damned, into the Light where your soul can abide in a place of eternal bliss. Azrael drags the others into the Dark, a place of eternal torment."

"So, does the person who dies choose or is their final resting place chosen for them?"

"I suppose in a way one always chooses their destiny. Our choices in life are played out in death."

"So this Warder wanted to escort you into the Light and you refused?"

Anne nodded. "I was cheated out of a life. All the men around me took my choices away from me. Once I was free of their control, I chose for myself and I chose a different way."

Saoirse opened the door and admitted the servant, who laid their veritable feast out on the small dining table. He handed Saoirse something in a leather enclosure. She opened it, wrote something in it, and signed it before handing it back.

When he left, Anne asked, "Do you not need currency?"

"No, they'll just add it to my bill, and I'll pay when I'm ready to leave."

"I have money. Your kindness should not be rewarded by incurring indebtedness on my behalf."

Saoirse dismissed her concerns and proceeded to introduce her to the various culinary delights in this century. Most of them had ingredients with which she was familiar—beef, vanilla, citrus, but never had she experienced them in their various forms. Anne was shocked when Saoirse cut one of the items in half—the cheeseburger—and ate it with her hands. Only peasants ate with their hands. Delicately she picked up the piece of meat and melted cheese between two pieces of bread and bit into it. The juice dribbled down her chin, but Anne didn't care. It was delicious. She quickly realized she was particularly fond of the cheeseburger and the crème brûlée—a vanilla custard with a hard shell of sugar on the top. Anne would have been hard pressed to determine her favorite.

Just as they were finishing, someone knocked on the door again. It was becoming less and less disconcerting. Saoirse opened the door, and a lovely woman with light brown hair streaked with silver and sunlight joined them.

"Anne, I'd like you to meet my old friend, Rachel Moriarty. Rachel, I'd like you to meet a new friend, Anne Hastings."

The color drained from the woman's face. "Not Hastings. Boleyn. Oh my God, how did you get here?"

Composed, Anne stood, and held out her hand. "I came from the Void, the place between life and death.

I escaped through the Veil early this morning as Big Ben struck three."

"The witching hour," whispered Rachel.

"I am no specter or spirit sent to haunt you," Anne said gently, for the woman looked as though she might faint.

"But why Hastings?" asked Rachel, the color beginning to return to her face. "I understand not using Boleyn as a last name, but why not your mother's name, Howard?"

"Because it was the Howard family who used my sister, myself and that poor, foolish child, Henry's fifth wife and the other one of us he had executed. That family's lust for power was second only to my father's. Their riches and titles were paid for in blood, mostly from the female line.

On September 1, 1532, Henry had me made Marquess of Pembroke in my own right. The family names most often associated with Pembroke were Tudor, which I obviously wasn't inclined to use and Hastings, which is even older than Tudor. I chose my own name when I made my way back to claim the life that was denied to me."

CHAPTER 5

*G*abe left his office and headed to the foyer to see Felix.

"I've got my people on board for this evening's activities. I assume we're still meeting for dinner. Has Saoirse arrived?" he asked.

"She has. She came in with a friend, and they went up to her room and ordered lunch. She didn't say a word to me. It was most odd."

"Well, Saoirse is a rather odd girl," Gabe said with a grin. "She probably had things on her mind. Or maybe the friend was in trouble and needed a shoulder to cry on."

"Could be. Pretty girl, but no luggage."

"Is she staying with us?"

"Not that I know of. It just seemed strange."

Gabe had learned a long time ago not to discount Felix's observations. On more than one occasion, the head concierge had spotted trouble long before it became an issue. He would just take a quick trip up to Saoirse's room to ensure all was well. He wanted to be able to reassure Felix in no uncertain terms that the beautiful Irish witch was fine. Just as he glanced at his watch, he noticed Rachael Moriarty headed into an elevator. Gabe doubted Moriarty would be her last name for much longer, and he smiled. There would be an awful lot of disappointed subs at Baker Street when they learned DSI Holmes was off the market.

But what was Rachel doing here so early?

He called the security center where members of his staff monitored activities throughout the hotel. They informed him that Rachel's elevator had stopped on the fifth floor. He walked to the front desk and confirmed that the fifth floor was where Saoirse's room was located. Interesting, especially given Felix's impressions of Saoirse's visitor. Deciding he'd go check up on them, Gabe headed for the bank of elevators.

He smiled as he walked down the hallway and saw how many guests, at least on this floor, were planning to participate in the Halloween activities this evening. Making a mental note to check the other floors, he knocked on Saoirse's room door.

"Oh, Gabe, I wasn't expecting you. Is there a problem?" Saoirse asked, being careful to only open the door enough to speak with him but preventing him from seeing inside the room.

"No. I just wanted to welcome you back to the Savoy, and I thought I'd also ask Rachel if she and Holmes were planning to come to dinner this evening?"

Saoirse wasn't a very good poker player. The surprise at his knowing Rachel was with her showed clearly on her pretty face. "Um, yes. Rachel is going to have Holmes meet her here."

"And your friend? I just want to make sure we ordered enough food."

Saoirse frowned, clearly and visibly annoyed that he knew exactly who was in her room. Gabe gave her his best reassuring grin. Saoirse needed to know there was little that went on in the hotel that he didn't know about.

Her voice remained even as she addressed his concerns. "It'll be fine, I'm sure. My friend Anne hasn't decided whether or not she'll join us. She's just gotten out of a bad marriage, and she may just want a bit of alone time. Do I need to let the front desk know she'll be staying with me?"

"Not necessarily, but if you need extra towels or bedding, just let the staff know. It's nice to see you again, Saoirse. Tell Rachel and your friend I said hello and look forward to seeing them later."

"Who was that?" asked Anne as Saoirse closed the door, still annoyed.

"Gabriel Watson. He's in charge of hotel security, and a really nice man," said Rachel. Shaking her head, she continued, "You're Anne Boleyn. I still can't believe it. I have so many questions, none of which are any of my business."

Anne laughed. "I have questions of my own. I am still finding it difficult to believe I managed to escape after all these years. I am almost afraid to close my eyes for fear that if I do, when I open them, this will all have been a dream and I will be back in the Tower."

"You said you thought someone or something might try to take you back," said Saoirse.

"I cannot believe that the Warder of the Veil or Azrael would be willing to let one of their charges slip away."

"Where were you exactly? I mean, I assume you were at the Tower," said Rachel.

"I was. I was in a place the Warder called the Void. I suspect I know far more about it than most, as he and I talked quite a bit over the centuries."

"What is it?" asked Saoirse.

"It is the place between this plane of existence and the next. At the Tower, as I understand it, when someone dies, their spirit drifts back to the place they were before their execution. How they lived their life determines who meets them. It's either the Warder,

who helps them to a place of eternal joy and peace—
the Light. Or it is Azrael, the Angel of Death, who
takes them to a place of eternal torment and darkness. I am sure, much to the surprise of many of my
contemporaries, it was the Warder who met me. He is
a kind and gentle soul and tries to comfort those who
are, understandably, distressed about being dead. He
guides them to the Light and sees them across, so they
are not alone. Azrael, on the other hand, gives those
who have died no time to reconcile themselves and
drags them to the Dark."

"But you didn't want to go into the Light?" asked
Rachel.

"No. I had determined before Henry had me
executed that I would try to find a way back."

"Why?" asked Saoirse.

"Because I was denied a life. From the time I was
a small child, my life was controlled and decided by
men with no thought as to what I might want or how
any of it affected me. At the age of twelve, I was
shipped off to the Netherlands. Please do not misun-
derstand—the Archduchess Margaret of Austria
treated me as well as my own mother. She was incredibly kind and generous. I was surrounded by books,
paintings, artists and men of great learning, but it
does not mean I did not miss my family or I would
not have preferred to stay at Hever with my mother
and siblings."

Anne sighed. "In 1514, I was sent to the Court

of France to serve Henry's sister. Again, no one asked me if I wanted to go. My father decided I should, and so I was removed from the second place I had been happy. When her husband died, Mary returned to England, but Queen Claude requested I remain. My father acquiesced and I was left behind. My sister joined me for a very short time but returned to England after destroying her reputation."

"She didn't do much better when she got back," said Rachel.

"No, she ended up in Henry's bed, encouraged by my father to do so as it meant advancement for him and our family. Their affair lasted longer than most. Mary was married and, therefore, could make no demands on the king. She had two children that the king never acknowledged, but they were his." Anne laughed bitterly. "Henry was quick to fuck someone's wife, but if he had an affair with them, their husband was denied his conjugal rights. Henry did not share his mistresses."

"He really was a bastard, wasn't he?" Rachel said.

Anne's brow wrinkled in confusion. "No. His parents were legally wed even before his older brother Arthur was born."

"Sorry. We don't use that term to refer to someone's legitimacy anymore, but rather to say that he was a tyrant and a monster."

"Ah!" Anne grinned. "Yes. In that case, Henry was

a real bastard. You know, I was never unfaithful to the king."

Rachel laid her hand on Anne's arm. "I don't think even during the trial anyone believed that."

"He murdered me, along with five innocent men, just so he could have Jane Seymour. I have never understood that. By then, he was the head of the church. Why not just divorce me? I shared Henry's bed for a little over three years and became pregnant four times. It is not my fault that only Elizabeth lived. His seed was weak, yet he blamed others for his inability to father a healthy son."

Leaning in, Anne studied the historian, curious. "I have heard talk of my daughter. Did she truly eclipse her father?"

Rachel nodded. "She ruled for more than forty years, and they call that time the golden age. She was a genuinely great monarch."

The thought pleased her. She allowed herself a small smile, though it was bittersweet because she'd been denied the chance to raise her daughter.

"I used to watch from my window when she would play outside at the Tower," she said. "When that bitch born to Catherine and Henry had her arrested and put in the Tower, I feared she would suffer my fate and determined that if it were so, I would try to keep her with me so we could escape the Void together. But she managed to evade all of Mary and Norfolk's traps and emerge victorious."

"That she did."

"Did Azrael ever try to force you to go into the Dark?" asked Saoirse.

"No, I was bound for the Light. On the night I escaped, he tried to chase me down to prevent it. I wonder if whoever it is that controls these things will not send him to try and bring me back, but the Warder may be the one they send. Or they may try to stop him."

"Did you get to know both of them?" Saoirse wondered aloud.

Anne laughed. "No. Only the Warder—and even then, not as well as you might think after almost five centuries. I got the distinct impression that his time spent as the Warder was some kind of punishment or a way to make amends for something he had done in life." She laughed again. "I know he had trouble understanding why I refused to go into the Light."

"I'm having trouble with that as well," Rachel said, leaning in with curiosity. "You famously said you would have given your life many times over to save the men who had been accused with you, but if that wasn't meant to be, you would gladly accompany them and spend an eternity with them in peace."

She nodded. "Yes, and if I could have saved them, I would have. But Henry needed to be able to justify executing me."

"Do you think he knew—that you were innocent, I mean?" asked Rachel.

"He had to have known. For all his faults, Henry was no fool. At best, he allowed himself to be persuaded I was guilty, but most likely, he knew everything that was going on. As much as Cromwell despised me and considered me a threat, he would never have moved against me without Henry's, at least tacit, approval."

Rachel sat digesting that for a moment, then looked over to her friend. "Saoirse, what do you think Gabe really wanted?"

"He wanted to confirm you were here and see if he couldn't get a look at Anne."

"Should I beware of him?" asked Anne.

Both women laughed.

"No," Saoirse explained, "he's a good man. But he's also good at his job, which means we're going to need to get identification and a good story for you sooner rather than later. Rachel, do you think Anne is easily recognizable?"

"I think if someone was a real student of Anne's history, and they sat and talked to her, they'd think she resembled her. But there's no way anyone is going to think this is Anne Boleyn. It would be hard for anyone to accept she somehow found a way back to the land of the living."

"Which begs the question, why is it so easy for you?" asked Anne.

Saoirse and Rachel looked at one another before Rachel said, "Because we've just recently had a run-in with something evil. Not that I'm saying you're evil," she added. "But this creature broke through, not exactly from the other side, but from where it had been trapped by a witch."

"What do you mean?" asked Anne.

"I have a business conducting small, personalized tours. You must have seen tours going through the Tower."

"Ah, yes. I thought you looked familiar," said Anne.

"On one of them, the group wanted to see the sites where a serial killer…"

"Who would kill grain? And why would that be a problem?" asked Anne.

"Oh, dear," laughed Saoirse, setting her fork down. "A serial killer is someone who murders his victims sequentially and in the same manner as the others. In this case, a man in the time of Queen Victoria. He killed and eviscerated five women over the course of seven months. He was never caught."

"How awful," said Anne.

"It was. He seemed to have disappeared the night he murdered his last victim, Mary Jane Kelly. When we'd finished at her lodging, I saw the door was open and went to close it. We're still not sure how, but we believe his last victim was a witch and managed to remain in, I guess, the Void and cast him into a mirror. The mirror cracked and he escaped, but somehow got attached to me."

"Are we in danger?" asked Anne as she sipped delicately from the teacup.

"No," Saoirse said firmly. "He terrorized Rachel for a week or so, but we were able to send him to Hell with the aid of the banshees."

Anne smiled. "A killer of women? I rather imagine the banshees liked that."

"My point is that just having had a run-in with the paranormal, it's a lot easier for us and our friends to accept that Anne Boleyn might have decided to make a life for herself, bided her time and come back through the Veil."

"How many people?" asked Anne.

"There are lots of people who believe to varying degrees. But I'm talking about a small group of seven friends who experienced it."

"So, why not let this Gabe person see me?"

Rachel inhaled deeply. "Because even though Gabe is a good and honorable man, he doesn't know the truth about Holmes, Felix or Roark."

"What is there to know?"

"About a year ago, they pierced the Veil and entered the real world, not from the Void, but from the pages of Sage's books."

"Were they summoned here?" Anne looked at Saoirse. "Did you summon them?"

"No. We're not really sure how Felix and Holmes got here, but Roark was the hero of Sage's books and when someone tried to murder her, he was able to break through and save her."

"What happened in the books, and do you not believe Gabe is trustworthy?"

Rachel shook her head. "Nothing like that. It's just before the whole Ripper thing, Gabe had never had any run-ins with the supernatural, and honestly there was no reason for him to know. As for Sage's books, the rest of the world remembers them with the characters that appeared to take their places. It's been a bit surreal for them, which is why I think they could help or at least be a friend to you. I'm also pretty damn sure Holmes will know how to get phony documentation that will stand up to scrutiny."

"Why? Is he a forger?"

"About as far from it as possible," Rachel said. "No, my fiancé is a Detective Superintendent with Scotland Yard, which is a large police force based here in London. So, if we're going to get the boys—and that's something of a misnomer—to help, we need a good cover story unless Anne wants to tell them the truth."

"I would rather not. I had no choice but to trust Saoirse, and she vouched for you."

"I told Watson you were just out of a bad marriage, which isn't far from the truth. We could embellish that by saying he was abusive, and you need to start over. Do you think you want to stay in London?"

"I had not really given it much thought, which sounds odd considering I have been thinking about if for almost five hundred years. Part of me wonders if I would be safer to run as far away as possible, and yet I feel London is my home and it is where I belong."

Saoirse mused, chin in her palm. "If you're talking about Azrael or the Warder, I wouldn't think geographical location would make much of a difference. And if it did, then they might be confined to the Tower. I don't think London would be the worst place for you. After all, you've already made a couple of new friends, and it's an easy place to get lost in the crowd if you need to."

"I think Saoirse is right. And if we get you identity papers, that will help get you other things."

"I am not penniless," said Anne, lifting her chin.

"No, but those coins are going to be hard to sell without provenance. Can I ask how you had them with you?"

"When I was arrested, I was sure Henry meant to dispose of me. I had determined if I was to die, I would find a way back so had coins and gems sewn into the hems and cuffs of a number of my gowns. Henry had already set his eye on that pasty-faced bitch, Jane Seymour, who was not that much younger than me. But Henry had decided he had to have another, younger queen he could breed sons on. That did not work out the way he planned. I rather imagine watching my Elizabeth take the throne and rule for as long as she did made him apoplectic. Serves him right."

"For what it's worth, most historians believe you were the wife he truly loved."

"And yet," she said, lifting her hair and showing her the ugly scar on the side of her neck, "he had me executed. Wolsey was right; I was a silly girl. I actually allowed myself to fall in love with Henry. I was a fool. Never again."

Saoirse closed her eyes and shivered. "I can't even imagine."

"Don't say 'never,' Anne. I'd hate to see you spend this new life all alone," Rachel said.

"Says the woman who just got engaged to the well-hung, hunky DSI," teased Saoirse. "And while there's a part of me that agrees in theory, I think, Anne, that you should do what feels right to you. After all, you're the one who created this new life for yourself."

At the knock on the door, all three women froze and looked toward it.

CHAPTER 6

*S*aoirse held her hand up as she walked to the door. Once again, she opened it just enough to identify the person on the other side. Her entire body relaxed as she recognized their visitor. Stepping back, she opened the door to allow an auburn-haired beauty with a lush figure to enter the room.

"All right," the woman said, her accent sounding odd to Anne's ears. "What are you up to, and how come I wasn't included?"

"Anne Hastings, let me introduce you to Sage Matthews."

"The author?" Anne said, rising from the settee and walking toward her, extending her hand.

"Well, someone has to be. And no one else seems to want the job, although why, I'm not certain."

"She's also married to a rather well endowed,

virile and handsome man, and they are fabulously wealthy," stated Saoirse as Sage rolled her eyes and Anne laughed. "And they live here at the Savoy."

"I think Saoirse is the most jealous about Roark, the aforementioned well-endowed man."

Anne liked Sage immediately. Truth be told, she felt more comfortable with these three women whom she had known less than a day than she had with ones she had known her entire life from the time before with Henry.

"Your accent? I do not recognize it," said Anne.

"US of A," replied Sage. "D.C. most of my life, then the Outer Banks of North Carolina. I live here now with Roark." Anne looked at Saoirse and Rachel, who nodded. "So, they told you. Hmm… that's interesting. You must have a secret as well…"

"No, more of a connection to the supernatural," explained Rachel. "I hope you don't mind. We wanted Anne to feel comfortable with us and with you."

"Are we keeping it from the boys?" asked Sage, excitedly.

"We thought we might. At least for a while, until Anne gets to know them. She hasn't had the best of luck with men," explained Rachel.

"Anne's just gotten out of an abusive relationship and is kind of on the lam. We were hoping Holmes could help us find a forger to get her some new identification."

"Oh good lord, don't do that. He'll get all official. You know how he is about the rules. I know lots of people from doing research. So, who do you want to be?"

Anne smiled. "I thought I might be Anne Hastings. It was not my former name."

"I like it," said Sage. "Very British."

Anne shook her head. "No. I am not going to lie to someone I believe will become a very good friend."

Sage looked at Rachel and Saoirse. "Look, Anne, if they were going to let you lie to me, it's because they are very concerned for you, which is enough for me to be concerned. I can live with the lie of your name and other particulars, just not the essence of who you are."

"Your friends spoke well of you, and I should have trusted them. I understand your husband, Rachel's fiancé and the fellow from downstairs all stepped out of a book. And additionally, that a killer named Jack the Ripper attached his spirit to Rachel to bind himself to this time and space."

"And you didn't go running from the room thinking them mad. Sounds to me like you've had a run-in with something paranormal."

"As I understand the definition of that word, I *am* the paranormal. I pierced the Veil between the Void and the living earlier today. My former name was Anne Boleyn."

She let that sink in for a moment, and when she saw how pale Sage had gone, helped her to the settee.

"Holy shit. Wait. Can I swear in front of a queen?"

"Trust me, I can swear with the best of them and in several languages," laughed Anne.

"How? I mean, you don't have to tell me."

"There is not much to tell. Shortly before my execution, I decided if there was a way to not go into the Light, some way I could wait until I found a way back to the living, I would—much to the consternation of the Warder of the Veil and his counterpart, the Angel of Death. I waited and I watched and tried to learn this new way of speaking. I felt All Hallows Eve was my best chance to escape, and I was able to elude both the Warder and Azrael, so I tried and managed to get through to the side of the living."

"I ran into her in the coin shop, and one thing led to another," added Saoirse. "I couldn't just leave her in modern-day London, so I brought her back to the Savoy with me."

"I have money," said Anne, "and jewels I had sewn into the hems of my gowns after my arrest at Greenwich. But had it not been for Saoirse, I would not have been able to exchange even the one coin I did."

Sage nodded. "Yeah, I'm sure they wanted identification and probably some proof of provenance before exchanging them. We can probably find someone who can help with the fake identification, but a fake provenance or selling without it would be difficult. The abusive relationship will get us past some of the hurdles… Oh wait, am I included in this?"

The other three women laughed. "Sage writes fiction and does a lot of research," explained Saoirse. "Much to her husband Roark's dismay, she often meets with people who have less than exemplary reputations."

"That's putting it mildly," said Rachel. "Holmes has had to get her out of hot water with the authorities more than once when she was someplace she wasn't supposed to be."

"Ah, yes, but now aren't you all glad I did? The best forger I know is Nina Oletta. She's mostly out of the fake identity business, but I know she's still willing to work for a woman who's looking to escape a bad relationship. I think having him cut your head off qualifies," said Sage. "And we can probably get her to come up with some kind of provenance for the valuables you brought with you and want to sell. The problem is, we'll need photographs."

"What is a photograph?" Anne asked, trying out the last word.

"It's like a painting, only it's completed immediately," Saoirse said. "Sage? Do you have your mobile with you? Take my picture, which is another name for a photograph, and show it to Anne."

Sage pulled her phone from inside her bra and showed it to Anne, focused the camera on Sage, again showing it to Anne and then clicked. Saoirse joined them on the settee. Sage opened her gallery app and showed Anne the picture.

"How wonderful!" said Anne. "Can you take mine as well?"

"Of course," laughed Sage, moving so she focused the camera on Anne and snapped her picture, turning back to show it to her.

Sage handed her the camera so she could get a closer look. "Truly, is that what I look like?" she asked, reaching out with her finger to touch the cheek of her likeness who stared back at her. She had never thought of herself as a great beauty, like her sister Mary. But the woman staring back at her was attractive and had no reason to feel as though she were somehow less because of it. The feeling was most like touching glass, but smoother. She could feel no temperature or texture as she might in a painting. Truly the ability to capture one's likeness was a marvel.

The camera vibrated and played the James Bond theme song, making Anne drop it in alarm.

"It's all right, Anne. It's just my husband. It allows me to speak with him, even when he's not in the room." Sage stepped away from them to answer the call.

"Hi, babe. I'm down in Saoirse's room. Rachel's

here as well. You're back early. [PAUSE] New girl? Yes, she's a friend of Saoirse. [PAUSE] I don't know if she's up to joining us. I was going to ask her. [PAUSE] We're not doing anything important. I was going to hang out a while unless you have something better for me to do…" Sage let the conversation hang on her end and then blushed before ending the call.

"He can track you down and talk to you over that device?" asked Anne.

"Yes. I call them electronic leashes and I refuse to be tethered by one," said Saoirse.

"You wait until you find that one man who makes you go weak in the knees. Roark just likes to know where I am. He's still a bit spooked by the whole Jack the Ripper thing," said Sage.

"He could command you to his presence?" asked Anne.

"He could, but it doesn't mean I'd do it," replied Sage with a playful grin. "Roark is dominant by nature, and he worries. He's fine with me being here, just wanted to check. But I'll guess someone has said something about Anne, and he was curious. He said to invite you to dinner."

Anne shook her head. "I would not want to impose, nor do I think I am ready to meet with others. I feel safe with the three of you, but my trust in men was limited in my former life and is nonexistent in this one."

"I texted Nina Oletta while we were talking," said Sage, standing and beginning to pace.

"Texted?" asked Anne, looking between her new friends for an explanation of the unknown word.

"Yes," replied Sage. "It's another means of communication. We need to come up with a story for her and begin to craft a new life for Anne."

"Once we get ID," said Saoirse, "we can look for better—and by that I mean not as concerned with legalities—coin and gem merchants who won't require provenance. There's so much to do."

Rachel leaned into the displaced queen—a woman out of her own time. "But if you don't come to dinner, it may make the boys suspicious. You need to know, Anne, even if they get suspicious—even if they figure out we're protecting you—even if they figure out who you are, they will never betray you. Never. If it comes down to a fight with this Warder or this Azrael fellow, they will fight for you," said Rachel. "I know, because they didn't know anything about me, and they risked their lives for me."

"I can stay here," Anne insisted. "Perhaps there are books I can read."

Sage laughed. "I'm afraid the only books we have handy are mine, and you are welcome to them…"

"I'm not sure she's ready for that," Saoirse said with true amusement.

"When people are trying to learn a new language, they watch television," offered Rachel. "We could show you how to use it. It's kind of like moving pictures of a play."

"Fascinating," said Anne.

"But you are also welcome to come to dinner with us. We can come up with a good enough story to pass muster," said Saoirse.

"I think she's best off to experience her first television with someone to explain things to her," Sage added. "Otherwise, it will seem crazy. And the boys would be the best ones to try the story out on, because if they can see through it or recognize Anne, we'll have a better idea of what we'll need," said Rachel.

"What if they do recognize me?"

"Then we come clean and tell them who you are..." started Rachel.

"Is that wise? I am not convinced that men are any more reliable in your century than they were in mine."

"Well, divorce is a whole lot easier, so generally monarchs don't create a whole new religion or cut off the heads of their queens." Rachel held up her hand. "I know your interest in the Reformation was a genuine belief, but Henry never gave up being Catholic. In my opinion, the only reason he started the new church was that it made it so the only authority he answered to was God himself."

"Why do you say that?" asked Anne.

"Because I'm a history professor who specializes

in the War of the Roses up to the end of the reign of your daughter."

Anne's face lit up at the mention of her daughter. "So, you know about Elizabeth? There were times I worried about her and tried to watch over her. I fear she was no more fortunate in love than I was."

"You loved Henry, didn't you?" asked Rachel.

"Very much, but I refused to be bedded and discarded as he had done with so many others, including my sister Mary." She gave a quick laugh. "My father and uncle were furious with me that I refused to let him have his way. At first, I thought if I had to be with a man ten years my senior and past his prime, I would only do so if I could be queen and raise my family to a new station." Her eyes took on a faraway look. "But as he courted me, he showed me such respect and such genuine affection that I came to love him deeply."

Rachel put her hand on Anne's. "He must have wounded you deeply. I've always thought that many of the others Henry murdered could have taken lessons from you in composure and dignity in the way you faced your death."

"I had no choice. I could have harmed my family further had I spoken against him. Besides, the way he cheated on me and only seemed to see my miscarriages as my failure and not as the loss of our child… He broke my heart," she said softly, ending in a whisper.

"Do you know much about what happened after you died?" asked Rachel.

Anne nodded. "I witnessed a great deal. I know my body was barely cold when he married Jane Seymour and his precious son only ruled for six years, and the child he shared with Catherine, Mary, ruled for five. My Elizabeth," she said proudly, "ruled for almost forty-five years."

"And it was considered to be one of the most glorious reigns in English history. She did you proud, Anne. If it's any consolation at all, I do believe you were the only one he truly loved. And forgive me, but he could be incredibly stupid and gullible."

Anne smiled. "He was played by many, and to be fair, I was one of them. I outwitted Wolsey, but I believed that Cromwell and I were allies. He played me for a fool."

"He came to believe if he defended you, it would cost you both your lives. Did you know Henry had six wives? He put Catherine of Aragon aside for you..." started Rachel. "Executed you and Catherine Howard..."

"The girl was a shallow, brainless child who thought her beauty would buy her out of anything," said Anne with a shake of her head.

"But your uncle thought she would buy him back favor with Henry. As you seem to know, Jane Seymour died giving Henry his son. Catherine Parr was more nurse than spouse. I think of the lot of you, Anne of

Cleaves faired the best. She never had to fuck him, she had tremendous autonomy, and he made her one of the wealthiest women in England."

"Yes, but even she never got to be truly free," said Anne.

"By the way, Nina sent me a text and she can see us tomorrow about ten. I told her to meet us here and that Anne is fleeing an abusive boyfriend and needs to start over with no ties to the past," said Sage. "What do you think, Anne?"

Anne offered her a gentle smile. "It is as close to the truth as I believe we can be. And the more I think on it, if you believe I will be safe with these boys of yours, perhaps it is a chance I should take. If nothing else, we might have a better idea of what pitfalls await me."

CHAPTER 7

*G*abe checked in with his staff spread throughout the hotel and with those who would be keeping an eye on things from the command center. Gabe chuckled—'command center' was a bit grandiose, but his people liked calling it that. It was simply a room with a large almost circular desk with a number of computer monitors on it. The person monitoring the screens could switch from one to another with the flip of a switch or movement of a mouse. There were also a number of computers recording data and images so they could be stored and reviewed if needed at a later date. There were no windows and only one exit with a door that was kept locked. Only those with the proper security clearance encoded on their key card could enter.

"Hey, boss," said Mazie, the newest member of his team. She was a bright, plucky girl with short dark hair she wore in a pixie cut. In many ways she was the caricature of what people expected from someone who worked all days with computers—glasses, slightly overweight in oversized clothes with a smattering of freckles. She had failed the physical fitness test to become a member of Scotland Yard, but she had a keen intelligence and was a crackerjack shot.

"Everybody checking in?"

"Yes, sir. It seems to be quiet except in the meeting rooms where all the kids are gathering. I think it's great that the Savoy is doing this."

Gabe nodded. "Me too, but I'm really thrilled by how many guests are participating, not just in letting their kids go trick-or-treating, but in giving away candy."

"And the fact that the hotel gave them the candy is so awesome."

"We figured that way we knew what was being given out and that they were roughly the same size. The bags were all sealed when we gave them out. It doesn't mean someone couldn't tamper with them if they wanted, but we felt it added a degree of safety."

"When do the festivities end?"

"Technically at midnight, but my guess is we'll see participation really drop off after nine and so we may well shut it down before then. I'll be in the hotel all evening and will be checking in. You have my cell if you need me. I'll be up in Roark and Sage's suite."

Mazie's eyebrows went up, and she leaned

forward with interest. "Any idea what her new book is about and when it's coming out?"

"I do, but I've been sworn to secrecy. Although I do have it on good authority that Sage is planning a little get-together for employees only, at just after midnight on release day… but you didn't hear it from me."

Mazie laughed. "Your secret is safe with me."

"Good girl. I'm going to head upstairs. Call if you need anything."

Gabe headed for the bank of elevators and rode up to Roark and Sage's suite. The couple were among his best friends, and he had been genuinely happy for both Roark and Holmes when they found the women of their dreams. He was beginning to wonder if it would ever happen for him. Would there come a day when he could share a life with someone—just jump into it together and face whatever came their way?

Like Holmes, Felix and even Roark, he was a member of Baker Street, the famed **BDSM** club in London. And like Holmes, he had begun to crave a deeper connection. At first, he told himself that the incident that ended his military career had put him off anything serious forever. Gabe laughed at himself. *I guess forever isn't as long as I thought.*

There had been a time he'd played at the club several times a week, usually with a different sub each night. Maybe that made him something of a manwhore, but he'd always been completely open and honest with any sub he played with. But ever since Holmes had found and collared Rachel, Gabe found himself watching his two friends and envying them their relationships. It wasn't that he fancied himself with Sage or Rachel, but more the deep and abiding love, commitment and dedication each man had found.

Gabe pushed these musings aside. Tonight, he was simply looking forward to an evening laughing and having dinner with his friends. All that changed when the door to the elevator opened and he heard a woman scream.

Instinctively, his fingers twitched, itching for a weapon, a holdover from his military days. It wasn't the first time he envied Roark's ability to carry a concealed weapon. He knew on more than one occasion, Holmes had wished he'd been armed, and Watson felt the same, but working the Savoy it was only rarely that he might need one.

He pushed on the elevator door, forcing it to open more quickly, and rushed out into the hall. He charged toward four women standing at the end surrounded by a group of teenagers, most of whom he recognized as guests at the hotel.

"It's okay, Gabe," called Sage.

His heartbeat easing at the reassurance, Gabe slowed to a walk and joined the group, more curious now than worried. He raised an eyebrow at the ladies questioningly.

"They just startled our friend," added Rachel.

"We're really sorry," said one of the boys, who Gabe recognized and who was dressed as some kind of grim reaper.

"No, it is my fault," said the most beautiful, cultured, English-accented voice he'd ever heard. "You startled me, and I have had a difficult week." She gave a small laugh. "My blood-curdling scream must have frightened you, and I do apologize."

"No. We thought you were our folks. We didn't mean to scare you," the young grim reaper said.

"No harm done," said the unknown woman.

Saoirse gestured toward her. "Gabriel Watson, this is my friend, Anne Hastings. Anne, meet Gabe."

It was at that precise moment that Gabe's life changed forever. The world tilted on its axis as the beautiful woman, who'd been standing with her back to him, turned to acknowledge his presence. He'd been about to admonish the boys to be more careful, yet now he found himself tongue-tied for the first time in his life.

The dark-haired beauty extended her hand and smiled. "Gabriel? Or do you prefer Gabe? I am Anne. My friends have told me so much about you. I am quite certain these strapping young men meant no harm, and I would ask that you not scold them or throw them in the Tower of London," she said, her eyes glistening with amusement.

"I'm not sure, Ms. Hastings," he said, going

along with her and enjoying every moment of it. "They look like brigands to me. I think the hotel, maybe even the city, might be safer if we locked them up."

The boys actually looked frightened for a moment, and Gabe relented. "I'm just giving you a bad time," he admonished. "But you guys be more careful, okay?"

"Yes, sir," said one of the boys.

"Thanks, Watson," said another.

The three boys ran down the hall and Gabe shook his head. "I am sorry if they frightened you…"

"As I said, I have had a difficult week and I fear I am not at my best. One of the lads, the tallest, had a horrible mask and reminded me of things best forgotten."

She moved subtly away from him, and he watched as her clothing clung and then fell away from what appeared to be a deliciously, curvaceous body. He was not a fan of the lean, hard bodies some women seemed to prefer to have these days. He wanted a woman with the kind of curves that invited a man's hand to rest there.

"Are you joining us for dinner?" he managed to ask.

"Yes, unless you would rather it was just the original seven of you."

A flush of excitement ran through him at the thought of spending more time with her. "No, not at all. The more the merrier, as they say. Besides, with you it'll be eight."

Duh, Romeo! He offered her his arm, which thankfully, she took.

Anne laughed. It was a delightful sound that rather reminded him of champagne cascading down one of those waterfall features people used at weddings and other festive events. He paused. Why had weddings leapt to mind? He'd only just met the woman. Surely, he couldn't be thinking of weddings because of her… or could he?

"Yes, the last time I checked, one when added to seven equals eight," said Anne.

"Come along, Watson," said Sage. "You can alibi us out with Roark."

He held up his hands in denial. "No way. The last time I did that, your husband wanted to punch me."

Anne arched an eyebrow. "I have yet to meet Roark, but I find it hard to believe that a man with your physical attributes would have anything to fear from anyone. Besides, as I understand it, you are the head of security and Roark is merely a guest."

Gabe smiled, feeling himself falling under Anne's spell, and not giving a damn. Perhaps the tall, black-haired beauty with the oval face and dark eyes was a witch like Saoirse. If that was the case, he hoped there was no cure for the spell she seemed to be casting.

He escorted the ladies down to Roark and Sage's

room, arriving just as Holmes stepped off the elevator to join them.

"Gabe? Who's your new friend? I don't remember her from Baker Street," said Holmes in greeting.

"I thought you'd forgotten about all the other submissives from the club," said Rachel with a bit of ice in her tone.

Holmes swept her up in his embrace, kissing her deeply and passionately until the tension left her body. Watching with a bit of envy, Gabe was beginning to hope that someday he might be able to kiss Anne out of a frosty mood. He wondered if she had any submissive tendencies or might be inclined in that way.

"I have my beauty," Holmes declared. "All others have faded into the mists of time, and only your image remains in my mind."

Saoirse, Sage and Gabe groaned.

"You'll have to forgive them," Gabriel said to Anne. "They just got engaged."

"Why would they need my forgiveness?" Anne retorted. "Rachel's fiancé was merely reassuring her of his love. In my experience, those who have to do so often are generally the ones who need forgiving."

Rachel regarded Holmes coolly and withdrew her arm, taking a step closer to Saoirse.

"Then you'll find Holmes and Roark to be the exceptions," Gabe said. "Both of them are nuts for the women in their lives and as far as I know, neither has ever so much as looked at another woman since he met his beloved."

"Sage, how long have you and Roark been married?" asked Anne.

"A little over a year."

"Time will tell. Men can often control their baser natures for a year, but if parted from their sweetheart for any length of time or if she becomes pregnant, everything changes, and we women are expected to put up with it," said Anne with some reserve in her tone.

Her back straightened, her shoulders moved back, and her overall body language became tense and wary. *What the hell was she hiding?*

"On that happy note, let's join Roark," said Sage, linking her arm though Watson's and leading him to the suite she shared with her husband.

Gabe could overhear Saoirse speaking to Anne behind him. "Not everyone is like Henry or the other men you knew. The men who will be here tonight are good, honorable men…"

"And Henry was named Defender of the Faith…"

The combination of Saoirse shushing her and Felix's arrival meant Gabe couldn't hear if anything else was said. The two men stepped aside to discuss Savoy business.

"Gabe, the evening is going fabulously, and your staff is doing an outstanding job," said the hotel's head concierge.

"Thanks, Felix. I was really proud of my staff. All of the people without kids volunteered to take shifts tonight so that the ones with kids could be with their families."

Felix nodded. "Same thing with my folks. Makes you feel like you're doing something right."

Gabe glanced across the hallway at Anne. "Who's the lovely lady with Saoirse? Have you met her yet?"

"She's a friend of Saoirse's. She's coming off of a bad break-up."

"I take it he cheated on her?" asked Gabe.

"Multiple times, apparently, so cut her a little slack."

Gabe stopped and looked back at the beautiful Anne. Cheated on? That seemed impossible. Of course, he'd cut her as much slack and time as she needed. There was something about Anne Hastings that called to him. It was if she had come from nowhere just to be with him.

Sage punched in the keycode and opened the door. "Hey, babe! I've got everyone with me."

"Damn, and I was planning to ravish you before they got here," Roark called back.

Sage rolled her eyes at Anne. "It's five to six. That man couldn't ravish me in five minutes if his life depended on it. He's much too good a lover."

Anne smiled and said nothing, but touched Gabe's arm. "I fear I owe you an apology. My most recent relationship ended badly, and I may have sounded a bit sharp."

Once more, Gabe tucked Anne's arm into his. "Not to worry. And for the record, I think any man who cheats on a woman he's involved with ought to have his balls cut off."

"What a perfectly charming attitude, Gabriel. I think you and I might get along quite well."

He gave her a winsome smile, delighted with her all over again. "Nothing would please me more."

CHAPTER 8

The evening had gone fairly well, Anne thought. The food had been delectable. She was coming to realize how different and limited the choices of food had been available during her lifetime—no, first lifetime—had been. Everyone seemed to have such courtly manners. No one talked with their mouth full or belched. And then there was Gabriel with his tall, strong physique, blonde hair and chiseled features. She allowed herself to wonder what it might feel like to run her hands over the hard planes of his body, to feel him part her thighs in preparation to make love to her. No, she thought, mentally shaking those thoughts from her mind.

Now that everyone had gone and she was back in Saoirse's room, the delicious supper she'd eaten was making her sleepy, and she felt ready to rest. She glanced at her new acquaintance. "Saoirse, I insist you let me sleep on the couch."

"I won't hear of it," the witch replied. "You're much taller than I am, and you haven't a good night's sleep in almost five hundred years."

Anne couldn't help but laugh. She was finding Saoirse and the other ladies she had met today to be good company. Even the men had seemed more trust-worthy than those with whom she'd been raised and spent her life.

"Tell me what you know about Felix and Gabriel," she said, adding Felix into the mix when it was only Gabriel that interested her.

"I'll tell you everything I know, but it isn't much. I've known Rachel for years, but only met the other four when Rachel ended up dealing with Jack the Ripper."

Shaking her head, Anne hugged herself and said, "That must have been terrifying. Not to even know such a thing existed and then to have it stalking you. I wonder if I am not placing all of you in danger. I think I could forgive Henry his executing me. He wanted a son, and in three years I failed to produce. He believed he had to have sons to inherit and continue the Tudor dynasty. But I will never be able to forgive his torturing Mark Smeaton and executing him and those four other men, including my brother, for his own vanity and so he could brand me a whore."

"I never have understood why people thought torturing someone was a reliable way to get at the truth." Saoirse shook her head.

"It was not about the truth. Torture is never about the truth. It is about getting someone to say what you want them to say so that you can do what you want to do. But Henry was a fool to pick poor Mark."

"Why do you say that?"

"Because if Mark was interested in sleeping with any of the Boleyns, it was not me. I did always think he rather fancied my brother, George. And that the king would kill Henry Norris, a man who had stood as his friend for so many years? Despicable and dishonorable. He had to have known Norris would never have betrayed him."

"Do you think he believed it?"

"That, I do not know." Anne shrugged. "I do know that Cromwell did a masterful job at making me look guilty—a far better one than I would have done presenting the truth of what he did to the monasteries, but then I always believed he had done so on Henry's instructions."

"Why do you say that?"

"Because Henry wanted money. And robbing those who told you that you were wrong made him far more popular with the nobles than if he had raised their taxes."

"Did you have this clarity of vision when you were with him?" asked Saoirse.

"Oh, how I wish. I might have lived, or at least not have allowed him to break my heart. No, my knowledge of all the wrong he did to me, to my daughter, to my family and to others has been gleaned over time. Although looking back, I have to wonder if I chose to be blind to all of his faults, which far outweighed his virtues."

"I hate to be practical, but how do you plan to live? I have a farm in Ireland, and you are welcome to live with me. It won't be the privileged life you're used to…"

"But at least I will be alive," teased Anne. "Have I thanked you for rescuing me today? I am grateful, but if that single silver penny was worth so much as I understand your modern-day currency to be, I shall not be penniless nor a burden on anyone. And if my cousin did not play me false, and if it still exists, then I have a small fortune waiting for me in the Cardinal's wine cellar."

Saoirse's eyes widened. "Wolsey's wine cellar? Here in London? Why would you hide something there?"

"Yes, it was at York Place. As to why, because the Cardinal and I were bitter enemies, and no one would ever think to look there for something to benefit me or my kin."

"I read about York Place. When Wolsey died, Henry claimed it for himself and renamed it White-hall Palace. Most of it burned to the ground and they built the Ministry of Defence over it, but Wolsey's wine cellar is still intact."

Anne leaned forward, eager to learn more. "Can we get access to it?"

"There are a lot of hoops to jump through…"

"Hoops to jump through?" she asked, confused.

"I'm sorry," Saoirse chuckled. "It means we have to get special permission. Luckily for us, Rachel knows people who might be able to help. But all the wine was cleared out long ago."

"What about the cradles that held the barrels of wine?"

"I suppose they might still be there. Let me call Rachel…"

"I swear, Saoirse, I believe you are almost as out of practice with *l'affaire d'amour* as I am."

Pausing, the witch lowered her mobile phone. "What do you mean by that?"

"Unless I am very much mistaken, and I do not believe I am, Rachel is most likely in the throes of passion with her very handsome husband, who did seem very much in love with her." She paused, considering what she'd witnessed over dinner with the others. "Both they as well as Roark and Sage seemed to have a different way of interacting with each other than I have watched over the years."

Saoirse nodded. "Yes, what they call a D/s or power exchange relationship. The D stands for dominance and the s for submission."

"I thought women had reached equal status with men."

"Depends on how you define equal. We're a lot closer than during your time, but in this case it is something they both want. Rachel says for her, being Holmes' submissive gives her a place where she can just be and not have to think about anything. She can let Holmes carry a lot of the burden of the relationship."

"What does he get?"

"I used to think sex on demand, and there is that, but I'm sure you noticed both Roark and Holmes dote on the women in their lives. They serve them in as many ways as Rachel and Sage serve them. Rachel once told me she gives Holmes the peace of dominance, while she finds the same in submitting. I used to think it was all fucked up, but I've been doing a lot of reading, and Rachel invited me to go to a club that allows couples and those not in a relationship to experience that in a more controlled setting."

"So, any man could just decide he wanted to have sex with you?" Things hadn't changed as much as she thought. The idea of going someplace to be used as a common whore was off-putting to say the least.

"No, not at all. The subs are protected, and it is all consensual. If the sub changes his or her mind, the Dom has to back off. If the Dom doesn't, there are monitors who step in. It's all about people exploring their limits and boundaries. It's kind of cool. If you want, I can show you some of the information I found."

That put a different spin on it. Anne pushed the intriguing thought away, shaking her head. "No. I swore I would never be under another man's thumb again."

"I know it's not easy but try not to judge all things through your own experiences," she encouraged. "Did Rachel or Sage looked bullied or ill-treated?"

"No, but still…"

"They chose for themselves. I don't get what Rachel gets out of letting Holmes spank her when she's broken the rules…"

"Better than cutting off her head for no reason, I suppose," said Anne.

"Exactly! But she does say it gets her incredibly aroused and does the same thing to him."

A sense of longing overtook her at the thought. How long had it been? It seemed forever. "God, I miss sex," she confessed.

"Well, we can probably fix that. Although if it were me, I'd be focusing on other things at the moment."

Anne walked to look out the window. "Perhaps. But you have not been without the touch of a man for almost five centuries. And for seven years, I kept Henry at bay and no man touched me." Her voice grew wistful as she remembered better times.

"The first year we were together, I learned to revel

in his touch. The way my body came alive was more intoxicating than any wine. But only he was allowed to touch me, to pleasure me. I understand that women have long ago learned to pleasure themselves." Anne turned back to Saoirse. "Do you pleasure yourself? Is that why you say you would focus on other things?"

A bit of red crept into the witch's cheeks. "Not sure I want to have this discussion, but I will agree, you've been doing without for a long time."

Determined to learn more, Anne persisted despite the other woman's comment. "You say this club could provide me the pleasure I want?"

"I'm not sure how it all works. I know that both Dominants and submissives have to take classes, be trained and pass tests to play at Baker Street."

"The men are trained to please their women?" Anne grinned. "This is an improvement."

Saoirse blushed and rubbed her hand across her forehead. "Yes, and a lot of other stuff. Anne, this is not my area of expertise. Sage would know far more about what's done there and how people are trained. I know there's a protocol about how people behave— both Dominants and submissives. Not all men are Doms; not all subs are women. But honestly, Rachel or Sage would be much better to talk to about this."

"I am sorry to have embarrassed you. But there is so much I need to know. Do you think Rachel will talk to us in the morning?"

"Yes, both she and Sage plan to be here when Nina comes to get your paperwork started."

She glanced toward the bedroom. "Are you sure I can't talk you into sleeping in the bed?"

"I am," said Saoirse. "Sleep well."

"You too," Anne said, turning to head into the bedroom. Then she paused, just within the doorway. "Saoirse?"

"Yes?"

Without turning to face her, Anne continued, "Do you know much about Gabriel?"

"I know he isn't married or even involved with anyone. I know he's a Dom with Master's privileges at Baker Street, although I'm not sure what that means exactly. I also know he seemed quite smitten with you."

Anne's laughter trickled back over her shoulder. "Now, that's the best news I have heard in a long time. And I am quite the expert in time's lengthy passage."

As she closed the bedroom door, she mused on the man she'd recently met. Gabriel Watson was intriguing, to say the least. He had been born in America, in a city called Chicago. Anne had a vague notion of where this country America lay and had been fascinated that they had risen up as a nation and cast off the shackles of the English monarchy. She couldn't say she blamed them. Gabe had said this America was much colder and hotter than England.

Alone now, and ready to rest, Anne slowly

removed her clothing. It had been such a long time since she'd done that. The sensations of fabric, and air, on her skin delighted her. Anne craned her neck from side to side, stretching as she did so. Being back among the living, she could feel again—all sorts of sensations that she now realized she'd sorely missed. In the Void, she had existed but had felt little. There were specific times each year her emotions surfaced, but mostly she had survived in a sentient fugue state— the birth of her daughter Elizabeth, the date of her execution, and a few others. All else had been a sort of blur.

She settled the nightgown Sage had given to her over her body. It was by far the softest thing she'd ever felt against her skin. And it was quite lovely too. She stood in front of the mirror. The gown was quite scandalous as it left nothing to the imagination; her breasts with her dusky areolas and stiffened nipples were visible and demanded attention.

It truly has been far too long. Anne stifled a quiet laugh. She hadn't realized that one of the things that would return so quickly, now that she'd returned to the land of the living, was her libido. With that realization and as she looked at her ripe body, she wondered if Gabriel might like to see her in the scandalous nightgown—or better yet, out of it. She wondered what he slept in—or better yet, what he looked and felt like naked.

He had the musculature of a warrior. His shirt

had fit him well, and she had felt the hard strength in the man's hands and arms beneath the sleeves of his shirt as he'd guided her safely down the hall to dinner. The way his pants fit indicated he had powerful thighs; the pant legs molded themselves to his buttocks, which appeared to be carved out of glorious stone. His shirt had been open enough to give her a view of his broad shoulders and sculpted chest.

Anne had caught a glimpse of a smattering of blond chest hair that matched the locks on his head. She imagined it would match the color of the nest of curls surrounding his cock. A cock which had looked impressive as it bulged against the front of his pants. Henry's had looked impressive too, but it had been disappointing to discover the appearance was mostly due to his cod piece. Gabe, though, didn't seem to wear a cod piece, at least not from what she could tell.

The veins in Gabe's forearms stood out in stark relief to his smooth, warm skin. She had to wonder if his cock had similar veining. And she longed to find out, tracing it with her tongue while she played with his balls.

Closing her eyes, Anne rolled her head back and allowed her hands to palm her breasts before rolling her nipples between her fingers and thumbs. She'd forgotten how good it felt to do that. Once she had caught the attention of the king, she had been forbidden to touch herself in anything resembling a sexual manner. Her fingers now brought into sharp focus how much she had missed being touched. Her body seemed to truly come alive—her skin warmed as her nipples pebbled into painful tips, and desire swirled in her nether region.

It felt wonderful and frustrating at the same time. Fortunately, she had a vivid imagination, and she allowed herself to consider how much better her body might feel if it was Gabriel's strong hands doing the caressing, instead of her own. She moaned, hoping Saoirse couldn't hear her.

If Saoirse was unable to answer her questions about Baker Street, she would need to learn more from either Sage or Rachel. Anne felt the most comfortable with Rachel, as the woman seemed to know her story and was sympathetic to all that had happened to her. But it was Sage who wrote the novels filled with erotic stories. If there was a place where she could control the encounter and get what she wanted without having to give more of herself than she desired to give, she wanted to know about it.

Anne crawled into bed, relishing the softness of the sheets. There had been nothing like this during her original life. Even the finest linens in the palace had been unable to match the luxurious feel of the bed she now lay in. She wiggled her toes, fluffing and arranging the pillows, delighted with this whole, new, decadent experience.

Next, she turned off the light, proud of herself that she had remembered how. She stretched out and closed her eyes. But she could not drift into sleep just yet. Her body continued to sing to her of its need. She had been so careful, once Henry had noticed her, not to touch herself in any way that brought about pleasure.

But Henry wasn't here. He was cold, dead and food for the worms, lying next to Jane Seymour. Rachel thought that Anne was the queen Henry really loved, but Anne knew it wasn't true. He had become obsessed with Anne when she had spurned his advances and told him the one thing no other woman had—no. His intrigue with her had died quickly.

Henry had chosen to be buried next to Jane, the only queen to give him a son. They lay together in St. George's Chapel in Windsor. Anne had no such dignity. Instead, her body had been crammed into an arrow box—because Henry had not thought or cared enough to give her a proper coffin. And he'd buried her in a nameless grave under the high altar in the Tower of London. Her body had been moved and given a more proper burial, but Henry had been long gone when that had happened. Anne knew the truth. Henry had loved no one but himself.

Now, Henry was dead. So were her uncle and her father, who both had spent time in the Tower, but in the end had walked away as free men.

But Anne was alive. She was gloriously alive, and she fully meant to enjoy the time she had stolen back for herself. She stretched out, spreading her legs and letting her fingers skim over her body, hitching up the nightgown and letting her finger glide across the outer lips of her sex. The sensitive flesh felt velvety, and she could feel her feminine juices beginning to leak out.

Anne dipped her finger inside, desire humming throughout her entire body. She grabbed the pillow, holding it in front of her face so she could bite into it and muffle the sound of her indulgence. She stroked her sheath and thought she might die from the pleasure that surged through her system.

As the pressure built, she stroked faster and faster, adding a second finger to fuck all the way to where her digits joined her hand. When she ground the heel of her hand against the little jewel between her legs, it was as if fireworks exploded through her body. Unable to hold back any longer, she screamed into the pillow to smother her response. The most lovely, tingling sensation washed over and through her system.

As the feeling dissipated, she basked in the afterglow and promised herself not to go as long without once again experiencing that glorious sensation. Anne hugged the pillow to stifle her laughter. God, it felt good to be alive.

CHAPTER 9

*A*nne was enjoying the loveliest dream. In it, she and Gabriel Watson were enjoying one another's erotic company. She could feel his body lying atop her, having made a place for himself between her legs. His hard cock was up inside her; he moved it rhythmically back and forth as he bruised her lips with hard kisses, his tongue exploring and dominating her mouth. There was nothing subservient or effeminate about the man; he was a dominant male in his prime. She could feel him drag his hard cock back until he was just barely inside her before thrusting in again. Over and over as she writhed in is arms…

"My lady," a soft voice whispered.

Anne tried to ignore the voice.

"My lady," it persisted.

Gabe prevented her from turning her head. He

was intent on claiming what was his. Anne didn't know that she agreed with his assessment, but she didn't care. She only wanted to feel him driving into her in a ruthless pursuit of pleasure.

"Majesty," the voice whispered a little louder— this time loud enough to penetrate her dream and make her fantasy lover fade away.

Anne sat up, aroused and frustrated. "What?" she snarled and then had to stifle a scream.

There before her stood the Warder of the Veil. A tall man with silver hair, a full beard and kind eyes, he was dressed as she had always seen him—a scarlet and gold tunic coming to his knees, with red hose ending in fine black leather shoes with ornamental buckles along the top. A Tudor bonnet on top of his head completed the outfit. Anne knew from her time in the Void that her daughter had added the white ruff at their neck to complete the outfit, but the Warder of the Veil had been in his position from almost the time of the Tower's creation. It wasn't until the first execution by Henry VII, Henry's father, who had first installed the Yeoman Warders at the Tower that he had adopted their uniforms.

Anne took a deep breath and reminded herself that he had no way of knowing what she had been dreaming.

"What are you doing here?" she asked softly, looking about.

He looked at her, a kind yet sober expression on

his face. "I've come to take you back through the Veil, and this time I will guide you to the Light."

"No."

"Majesty, you have no choice. You do not belong here."

"That is where you are wrong. I did not deserve to get my head cut off because Henry wanted to fuck Jane Seymour."

"He was doing that before he executed you. Didn't you tell me that you'd caught them together, and it had upset you so much that you'd miscarried a son?"

Pain wrenched through Anne's body. She had suffered three miscarriages—two of which had certainly been boys, including the last one. There was a lingering guilt she felt about him because she had not grieved his death so much as feared how Henry might retaliate. After all, he had put Catherine of Aragon aside after her miscarriages once he had fallen for Anne. She had feared that now that his affections lay with Jane, he would do the same to her. And he had.

"That bastard was the cause of all my woes, including my execution and the loss of my babies. I am owed a life, and I will have it."

"Nay, Majesty. None of us are owed anything in this life. That yours was cut short by a capricious king does not entitle you to another. I had hoped over time you would choose to go into the Light when you saw escape from the Void was not possible."

"But it was possible. I am here."

"You cannot stay. You must return with me."

She stiffened. "No."

"Majesty, I implore you. The powers that control all that ever was or will be again will not allow you to stay. I begged them to let me come for you."

"I will not go."

"You do not understand…"

A rush of anger went through her body. "What is it you think that I do not understand?" she demanded. "That I was forced into a marriage I never wanted? That I endured all that being Henry's queen entailed? That I was impregnated repeatedly only to suffer three miscarriages? That I was executed on charges of treason and incest—charges which everyone around me knew to be false?"

The Warder shook his head, his gaze soft, concerned. "They will not allow you to stay. You must return to the Void. Once you are there, I can protect you from Azrael."

"I have nothing to fear from him…"

"He is not an entity that is easily defeated."

"But he is trapped inside the Void…"

"No. They will release him into the world to drag you back. He'll do whatever it takes to return you to the other side. And when he does…"

A chill ran through Anne and she gathered the

bedclothes around her, but she suppressed it, not willing to admit anything close to defeat. She watched him warily intending that he not step between she and the door into the other room.

"You assume he will find me and be able to take me back. He tried to stop me when I escaped, and he was unable to catch me."

The Warder made no move. He simply stood regarding her with sad and tired eyes. "You were very lucky. Had he caught you, he could have done what he will do now when he finds you. He will drag you into the Dark, to an eternity filled with torment. You deserve to be with those who love you in the Light."

"I will not go back. I will fight you…" Anne said defiantly.

"It is not me you need to fight. I cannot force someone into the Light, which is why you have existed in the Void for almost five centuries. I would not let Azrael have you. If you don't come with me or return on your own, you will be condemned to the Dark."

Anne thought for a moment, and then shook her head. She couldn't help noticing the sadness that seemed to descend over the Warder. "I waited almost five centuries. I waited until there was a time that as a woman I could control my own destiny. I am willing to risk it."

"Azrael will not be denied. He won't stop coming after you and if he has to, he will destroy those around you. They will give you some time to change your mind…"

"How much?"

"That, I do not know. But you will not have long. You do not belong here, and your presence raises the vibrations in this realm. If you do not return, they will unleash Azrael on the world. Please, Majesty, return with me and let me take you into the Light."

The Warder's words were passionate, and Anne knew he meant them. But she would not be persuaded to give up her last chance at a free life. "I will not," she said, her voice quiet but firm. "I have waited for my chance. I escaped the Void. I deserve to have the life that was denied me."

"If you change your mind, come to the Tower— to the same portal you escaped from—and I will meet you there to ensure Azrael cannot claim you. I beg you to reconsider."

"No. I will take my chances."

"You will not triumph," he insisted. "You will be forced to return. Your only choice is whether you go to the Light or into the Dark."

"No, Warder. I know you want what you think is best for me, but I will not allow others to choose my destiny. I will choose my own."

"And damn the consequences?"

Anne nodded. "And damn the consequences."

"Fare thee well, Majesty. I will wait and hope you change your mind before it is too late."

"Farewell, Warder. Know that I have always appreciated your kindness."

Anne watched as the Warder's image began to fade away. She drew her knees up to her chest and tried to stay awake. In the Void, she had never felt the need to sleep. Now she wanted nothing more than to lie down, close her eyes and wake to a new day, a new life.

Gabriel woke the next day to the same raging hard-on with which he'd gone to sleep. He'd thought about jerking off, but it had felt... unseemly. His arousal wasn't just a case of not having gone to Baker Street in a while. No, the cause of his erection had a specific name and face. Gabriel had been absolutely tongue-tied in front of Anne, and hoped he hadn't made too big a fool of himself.

Things hadn't been the same since Holmes had met and fallen in love with Rachel. It wasn't that he begrudged his friend finding his perfect match; he didn't. But it did make him feel like a bit of a third wheel. The two had become close when Sage had first entered their lives. They had often gone to Baker Street together, playing or sceneing separately, but having a drink afterwards. Holmes had become his best mate, and he missed some of the talks and fun they'd had together.

But he understood—now, more than ever. He'd wondered how Holmes had fallen so quickly, but when he'd seen Anne's face for the first time and looked into her dark eyes, he'd been entranced. Going home and getting ready for bed, he'd been able to imagine a whole life with her. He tried to dispel the feelings that were getting steadily stronger, but it was an utter failure. If anything, he felt more strongly about her this morning than he had when he'd gone to sleep the night before.

He glanced at his great grandfather's pocket watch he'd had made into a small bedside clock. If he got his ass in gear, maybe he could see her before he began his workday. He could get her room number and check to see if she had requested a wake-up call. If so, he would place it himself. If not, he'd figure out something else.

Gabe's family had been disappointed when he'd been forced out of a promising military career. His move from Chicago to New York to work in hotel management had been a bit of a relief—out of sight, out of mind. He knew they didn't tell their friends the specifics of his life only that he had moved to New York and then taken a job and moved to London. He spoke every year to his family on their birthdays and again at Christmas, but they seemed content that he had settled in Great Britain. He couldn't wait to speak to them during the holidays this year and tell them he was getting married.

Married? Where the hell had that come from? He hadn't even asked the woman out, and already he was daydreaming about spending the rest of his life with her.

His daydreams might be romantic, but his night-time dreams had been filled with the most righteously wicked sex. In his dreams, Anne had been the perfect submissive and a wanton firecracker. Perfect, of course, was a relative term. One of the first things he had learned in the lifestyle was that what one person considered perfect could be the complete opposite for someone else. He knew what he wanted—but Anne might have other ideas entirely.

He looked around his elegant one-bedroom apartment. The sitting room and kitchen were open concept. There was a large fireplace, over which hung a broadsword. The doors into his bedroom were antique French doors that he kept open and the entire end wall—both in the sitting and bedroom were of glass, affording him a tremendous amount of light. It was perfect for him—close to work, easy to maintain and in the best part of town, in terms of his needs and preferences. But could Anne be happy here? If not, they could find a place together.

Surprised by his thoughts, Gabe shook his head. What the hell was wrong with him? The idea of getting married, of uprooting his life, of giving up his perfect flat should have filled him with dread. And yet all he could feel was a kind of hopeful jubilance he hadn't enjoyed in a very long time.

Over the last couple of years he'd scened with subs. Gabe had never held any interest in pursuing a relationship with any of them. He was considered an excellent Dom, especially in the area of discipline and punishment. Before Holmes had gone off and fallen in love, Gabe hadn't given a thought to finding love. Rather, he'd had several subs he'd given discipline to on a regular basis. He hadn't had sex with them; he tried to keep the two separate, but Anne had him thinking otherwise. She'd proven to have a wicked sense of humor and had teased all of the men last night mercilessly—pulling back just this side of being rude.

He was well trained in the art of discipline. It was something he enjoyed, not from a power or pain standpoint, but it made him feel like he mattered. He loved his job and knew that the Savoy's management felt he and Felix worked well as a team to keep guests safe and happy. But he also knew some of the subs he gave discipline to felt he had improved their lives or curbed bad habits. He enjoyed discipline—both when giving it and in seeing the results.

What he realized he was missing, once Holmes had settled down, was taming a woman not only to submit to his discipline but to his will and to glory in that gift to him.

Anne was strong-willed, defiant, arrogant, stunningly beautiful and the most intriguing person he'd ever met. One of Gabe's strengths, both as a Dom and as head of security, was being able to size people up quickly and accurately, but Anne had proved something of an enigma—a mystery he wanted to solve.

Gabe shook his head, trying to break his own reverie. He knew so little about her. He didn't even know if she knew anything about the lifestyle, much less if she had any experience or interest in it. She wasn't a classic submissive like Sage or Rachel, and she would be more of a challenge to direct and persuade. She would keep him on his toes for the rest of his life… and he was looking forward to it. Gabe rolled out of bed and headed into the shower, letting the cold water hit his body with a shock.

He looked down at his hard cock, jutting out and up. Didn't the damn thing know it was supposed to retreat, shrink and soften in cold water? In response, it dripped pre-cum. How the hell was he supposed to spend any time around her if he had a continual hard-on? He might want a relationship with her, but his cock just wanted to get laid. Washing in barely tepid water did little to fix the problem. Nope, there was only one thing that would do that.

Gabe grasped his cock and began to stroke from the base out to the bulbous head. He had to get himself, his thoughts and his unruly cock under control. *No*, his body said, he needed to get his cock up inside Anne and the sooner the better.

He shook his head, throwing droplets of water from his hair onto the inside of the shower stall. Hoping to get finished quickly, Gabe closed his eyes and called forth the image of Anne—what she looked like, what she felt like, what she smelled like. He grinned as he realized she smelled like the aromatic bathing products the Savoy provided to guests.

It had been a while since he'd relieved himself this way, but the mere thought of Anne made it imperative that he pleasure himself. Gabe began stroking himself faster and harder, imagining it was Anne's pussy that was applying the pressure all up and down his staff. The thought was intoxicating.

He let himself envision what it would be like to have her spread wide, desperate for his cock, as he pounded into her. She would try to wrestle control away from him, but she would fail. He would hammer her sweet, wet heat, forcing orgasm after orgasm from her as she screamed his name. At some point he'd fuck her face-to-face and let her rake her nails down his back, but first he'd have her on her knees and take her from behind in the most male dominant position. He would leave her with no doubt as to who was in charge.

He could easily fantasize an entire scene in which she was face down over his knee, getting her pretty bottom turned bright red before he took her, pressing his cock inside her, reveling in her desperate, begging moans as his groin slammed into her backside each time he thrust deep. He would fill her with his cum, and it would drip from her when he was done. Groaning, Gabe felt his cock begin to spew semen onto the floor of the shower. He pumped until he was dry and then made quick work of cleaning himself and the shower.

If he was going to turn his fantasies into reality, he needed to get a move on.

CHAPTER 10

*a*nne was just waking up as Saoirse poked her head in.

"You're really here," Saoirse said with a smile. "Good morning. Did you sleep well?"

Anne stretched her arms up and over her head. "I did. Please tell me you at were at least somewhat comfortable on that couch. I should probably get my own room."

"It's actually quite comfortable, and I've given quite a bit of thought to that. Rachel and Sage will be joining us before Nina gets here. Why don't you look at the room service menu on the desk in the other room while I get dressed? Rachel's planning to bring you something to wear. We might want to take advantage of the hotel's shopping service, or we can go out."

"I think it would be best if I stayed close to the

hotel until I have identification and feel a bit more like I know what I'm doing."

"I agree, but I didn't want you to feel trapped."

"I will let you have your privacy and go look at the menu."

"It shouldn't take me but a minute to grab a shower and get dressed. I'll order breakfast and we can get started on constructing your new life."

Anne rose up from the bed, trailing her hand along the sheets. "It was the best sleep I have had in centuries," she teased.

Saoirse laughed. "I'll bet. If someone knocks, it's probably Sage or Rachel, but look through the little window in the door I showed you just to make sure. Do you remember how to unlock it?"

"I do. You must think me a fool for having to learn things children of your time know how to do."

"I think that you are a woman whose life was cut short and who defied the odds and found a way back. I think you are extraordinary."

Anne could feel heat suffuse her cheeks. When was the last time she had blushed? Saoirse had opened the heavy drapes and the morning sunlight filtered throughout the room. Anne was amazed when she stood at the window at all the activity. She had always thought of London as a vibrant place to live, but nothing in her former life compared to the hustle and bustle of the street below and the city that lay just outside her hotel room.

"Thank you. I fear I would have been lost had you not stepped in yesterday morning." She shook her head. "Hard to believe it was only yesterday. In some ways I feel I know you, Sage and Rachel better than anyone I ever knew."

"I'm glad. I feel the same way, and I believe Sage and Rachel do as well. So, I'm afraid you're stuck with us."

With a smile, Anne left the room and found the menu. She looked through the selections, not knowing what all of them were, but thinking they all sounded wonderful. Perhaps she'd ask Saoirse for her suggestions. Rising, she crossed the room and opened the curtains to bask in the warm sunlight. Looking at the Thames as it flowed by made her shiver. The last time she had traveled on that cold river, she had been under arrest and on her way to the Tower to await her death.

Her dark reverie was broken by a knock on the door. Anne could hear the shower still running, so she went to the door and looked through the little hole within it. The glass seemed to distort what she could view on the other side, but she could still see well enough to recognize that it was Gabriel Watson standing in the hallway. Eager to see him, Anne pushed her hair away from her face and unlocked the door.

"Good morning, Watson," she intoned, ushering him in.

He entered carrying a tray with two teapots, mugs and an array of muffins and scones. It all looked delicious, and Anne's stomach growled gently.

"I didn't know what you ladies would like for breakfast, but room service said you hadn't ordered anything," Gabe explained, a charming smile gracing his face. "I wasn't sure if you would be dining in or going out for breakfast, but I took the liberty of bringing you up a little something. I know Saoirse drinks tea, but I wasn't sure if you liked coffee so brought a pot of both."

Coffee? That had not existed in her time. Was he trying to trip her up? Gabriel Watson seemed like a highly intelligent man and she wondered if he knew there was something amiss in her story. The scent of the liquid in the other teapot was intriguing. Anne wondered if it tasted as good as it smelled. Not knowing the proper way to drink it, she decided it was better to experiment with it when she was alone or just with her friends.

Hoping to cover her ignorance, she returned his smile and said, "That was kind of you. Did you sleep well?"

"I did. I must say, you figured heavily in my dreams," he said with a wink.

He was awfully bold for a courtier she had only met the day before. Not courtier, she reminded herself, just a man. But perhaps a man who was feeling more comfortable in her presence than he should. His words and actions indicated sexual interest. She had always enjoyed courtly love, but she sensed there was danger in flirting with Gabriel. She might give away too much.

"Really, Watson, is that the way you always speak to a lady?" she chided.

He set the tray down. "It's the way I talk to a beautiful woman that I'd like to spend time with."

"Based on that bulge in the front of your pants, I am not sure the kind of time you would like to spend with me is something you should suggest to a lady of such a short acquaintance."

Gabe chuckled. "Interesting attitude from a woman who invites me into a room dressed only in a nightgown that leaves nothing to the imagination and whose body seems to have responded quite favorably not only to my presence but to the idea of spending that kind of time with me."

Anne looked down and realized not only could he see her naked body through the sheer nightdress but that he was quite correct about her body's appearance. Her nipples had stiffened in response to the idea of spending exactly the kind of time he had been suggesting. But to have pointed it out so bluntly?

"You churlish knave!" she hissed, pushing past him, going into the bedroom and slamming the door behind her to the sound of his laughter.

"Anne?" called Saoirse from the bathroom. "Are you all right? Did I hear someone?"

"Yes, and yes. Gabe brought us some refreshments and did not avert his eyes when he saw I was practically naked."

Anne paced back and forth in front of the window, trying to dispel the emotions churning inside her. That was one thing she'd always envied of Catherine of Aragon; that woman had always been in control. On more than one occasion, Henry had chided her for her outbursts or temper.

"Welcome to the twenty-first century," said Saoirse as she entered the bedroom. "I probably should have said something and had you put something on. Knowing Gabe, he didn't say anything insulting, but did enjoy the view. The thing to keep in mind is that while he might enjoy looking, he's used to seeing naked or practically naked women at Baker Street."

"Are the men in the same state of undress at this club?" asked Anne.

"Doubtful. As I said, most of the Doms are men, and men generally prefer to look at naked women." Saoirse finished dressing as she talked.

Anne rolled her eyes. "Honestly, some things never change."

"Grab one of the robes. He won't be able to see through it. Did you see anything on the menu to tempt you?"

"Had I known what more of the items were than I did, I might have found a lot of things I wanted to try, but it is difficult to know what to choose when you don't know."

"No problem, I'll order an omelet and some French toast. I like both, and you can taste both and decide what you want. And if you don't like either, we'll figure something else out."

"That sounds good. Should we order for Gabe?" Anne said as she walked back toward the sitting room.

"Uh, Anne?" Saoirse pointed at her clothes. "He can still see through that gown."

"Good. Let him look. If he behaves himself, at some point I might even let him touch me." Anne didn't wait for the other woman's response. She simply drew herself up, spine straight and regal, and returned to the sitting room.

"I expected you to cover up before you came back," he said with a smile, not bothering to hide the way his eyes swept over her appreciatively.

"And I decided this is my room, or at least Saoirse's, and that if you choose to put yourself in my presence without an invitation, you are responsible for how uncomfortable seeing me nearly naked is making you."

Watson surprised her by laughing. "*Touché.*"

"You might want to put your eyes back in your head, Gabriel," said Saoirse as she joined them.

"Hey, she said I could look, and let me just say, I have seen few things as beautiful."

Anne tried to maintain her stern look but failed

and found herself laughing with him. "You, sir, are terrible. Give me your jacket until Rachel and Sage get here with some clothes for me."

Gabe stood, removed his jacket and held it up to her. Anne knew his game. In order to put it on, she'd have to come closer to him and he'd get a better look. Truly, men hadn't changed much in five centuries. That was good news—Anne was good at playing men.

"I think, Gabriel, you are a brigand," she said, slipping one arm into the sleeve of his jacket and turning her back on him, holding her hair to one side so he could finish helping her into the garment.

"I see your opinion of me is improving. I'm quite sure a brigand is better than a churlish knave."

Anne laughed. "You are quite impossible."

She joined Saoirse on the settee as she poured tea. "Anne, would you like tea or coffee?"

"I would love a cup of tea."

"I'd like coffee," said Gabe, heading for one of the chairs opposite the sofa.

"I didn't ask you," retorted Saoirse. "Don't you have to get to work?"

Gabe put his hands over his chest melodramatically. "You wound me, milady."

"Out, Gabriel," ordered Saoirse as Anne laughed.

"You're going to let her just toss me out on my ear without my jacket?" he asked Anne.

"It's her room, but it doesn't seem quite fair,"

Anne said, starting to stand to remove his jacket and return it to him.

"Don't. He's just trying to get another look at your boobs. I know for a fact he always keeps a spare shirt, trousers and jacket in his office as well as several ties. Out." There was a knock on the door. "That'll either be the girls or room service. Tell me, Gabe, do you want Anne to give you back the jacket so that the guy bringing our breakfast sees Anne in all her naked glory?"

Gabriel made a growling sound as he turned, stalked to the door and allowed the server in. He waited as the young man placed their breakfasts at the small dining table and withdrew.

"Anne? Are you free for lunch?" asked Gabe from the doorway.

"No. She'll be busy."

"How about dinner?"

Before Saoirse could answer, Anne replied. "If you are offering to take me to dinner, Gabriel, I would like to go if you promise to behave like a gentleman."

"And if I don't?"

"Then I shall have something to look forward to, will I not?"

Gabe pulled the door behind him as he heard Saoirse's shriek of frustration.

"Looks like your date is raring to go," said the waiter as they walked down the hall.

Gabe stared at him. "I'd watch your mouth if I were you," he said, the words hard and sharp. "Anne Hastings is a lady, specifically my lady, so pass the word. And more importantly, she is a guest of this hotel. I don't think you want the chef or the head concierge to hear you were casting disparaging comments about her."

"No, sir," stammered the young employee. "I didn't mean anything by it. She's awfully pretty and I didn't know…"

"Well, now you do," admonished Gabe as the elevator doors opened and they both entered.

When they reached his floor and the doors opened, the poor waiter couldn't get off the elevator fast enough. Gabe would have to remember to reassure him in a few hours when he'd had time to stew in his own juices. When he reached the lobby, he headed to his office where, as Saoirse had correctly pointed out, he kept extra clothes in case he needed to change. He closed the door behind him and was a bit surprised when there was an immediate knock.

"Come in," he called, opening the door to the antique armoire to grab a different jacket. And, he admitted to himself, to hide his growing hard-on.

The idea that an almost naked Anne was upstairs wearing the clothes he'd been wearing did things to his thinking, and his body, that it shouldn't. All the blood rushed from his brain, rendering him incapable of coherent thought, and filled his cock, causing it to tighten. No doubt about it, he had, in the blink of an eye, begun to have deep feelings for the beautiful, haughty—dare he say regal—mystery woman who was sharing Saoirse Madigan's room.

Felix entered, closing the door behind him. "What happened to your jacket?"

"I loaned it to Anne," he replied casually as he pulled on a fresh one and turned to his friend and coworker. Gesturing toward one of the room's chairs for Felix to take, Gabe himself took a seat behind his desk.

"Why would someone at the front desk need your jacket?"

Gabe laughed. "She doesn't. I loaned it to Anne Hastings upstairs. Apparently, Sage loaned her a nightgown that—trust me—leaves nothing to the imagination. She asked to borrow my jacket, and as I don't fancy other men ogling her, I gave it up willingly."

Felix smiled knowingly. Gabe seemed to have developed a keen interest in the strange woman upstairs—and not in a head of security kind of way. "I wondered about that last night. She's quite lovely, a bit odd, but lovely. Roark and Holmes both think so too."

Gabe nodded. "As do I, but I don't think it's illegal

or odd that she's here. I don't think she presents any threat to the hotel."

"Neither do I. Saoirse called down and said she thought she and I should play chaperone. I understand you're taking Anne to dinner."

"I am, and I don't need Saoirse butting in." Gabe said, crossing his arms. Who the hell did Saoirse think she was... more to the point, what did she think he might do? After all, it wasn't as if he was planning to ravish Anne—fantasizing perhaps, but not planning. "Why don't you take Saoirse to dinner? Alone."

"I don't think Saoirse sees me as a romantic partner," Felix said a bit crestfallen. Gabe felt for the guy, it was obvious he was wildly attracted to Saoirse; his friend had a lot to offer a woman—especially one who was in serious need of boundaries.

"I think you're wrong. But if you're not, change her mind."

"We're not really suited. I'm a bit too conservative for her."

"Felix, have you never heard the phrase, opposites attract? The one thing I don't want is Saoirse running interference."

"You're sounding a bit fierce for a man who just met a woman the night before and knows next to nothing about her."

Gabe barked a laugh. "I know. It's the damnedest thing. I used to give Holmes shit about falling so hard and so fast for Rachel. He'd always say, 'when you know, you know.' He was right." He shook his head. "I actually woke up thinking about being married to her this morning, and it's taking every ounce of my willpower not to go look to see what Boodles has in rings and collars."

Felix sat back, eyebrows raised. "Is she in the lifestyle?"

"I have no idea. All I know is that I came into work this morning knowing I wanted to pursue something with her. I want to tame that wild spirit I sense lies under her regal presence, bring her to heel and spend the rest of my life with her. Oh God, I'm beginning to sound like Holmes." He shook his head, still shocked at his own reactions to the beautiful Anne.

Felix studied his friend, eyes crinkled in amusement. "Is that such a bad thing?"

CHAPTER 11

*a*nne sat with Saoirse, eating a delicious breakfast that made her grateful to be alive again. Breakfast in the Tudor era had been sparse by comparison—beer and bread, maybe a little beef—nothing at all like the sumptuous feast laid out before her. Anne was discovering she had quite the sweet tooth. The French toast might be bread, but Saoirse had explained it had been soaked in a mixture of eggs, cream, vanilla and cinnamon, which given its rarity in the age of the Tudors made it seem fairly decadent for an everyday breakfast. The other ladies had arrived, and now they talked as they awaited the person who would help her with identification documents.

"Apparently, Saoirse believes I am in need of a chaperone. She asked Felix to accompany her to dinner with Gabriel and I," said Anne, her eyes dancing with merriment.

"Don't you believe it," said Rachel. "She's merely using you as a way to get Felix to go to dinner with her without having to actually ask him."

"Not true. You didn't see the way Gabe was looking at her…"

"Rather like a hungry lion, looking to gobble up his prey," supplied Anne. "But we shall see who devours whom." Rachel, Sage and Saoirse exchanged looks. "What is it?"

"I know I mentioned this to you but… keep in mind that Roark, Holmes and Felix all stepped out of the pages of Sage's books. But only they and the people in this room know that secret," said Rachel.

"What about Gabriel?"

"He doesn't know. No one but this small circle is aware of the truth. Somehow when they appeared here in the real world, it was as if they had always been here and had always been known by those around them."

"You mean Gabriel believes he has always known them?"

"Not always, but for years. He and Holmes share common memories—ones which Sage never wrote."

Anne marveled at it all. It sounded so much like magic. And yet, here she sat eating scones after having crossed the Veil. How remarkable it all was.

"They do have another friend, a character in the

books, Eddy—he's a hacker and technological phenom," added Sage.

Anne laughed. "I have no idea what that means."

"I'm so sorry. In short, he's very smart and is able to manipulate all of our modern technology, like the mobile I showed you yesterday. A lot of what we do in our modern lives leaves an electronic trail from this tech, and Eddy is a genius at tracking it."

"Why is Eddy not out in the real world?" asked Anne.

"Because he doesn't want to be."

"And yet they remain friends... How do they communicate with him?"

"They found a special email address that seems to work in both realms—real and book. They send messages back and forth. I know all three of them urge him to come out, but so far he has refused."

Anne wondered about that word, *email*, but she decided not to ask. There was so much to learn, but for now, she wanted to concentrate on the immediate tasks at hand—getting her documents, and dinner with Gabe.

"Not to change the subject, but Nina should be here at any time," Sage noted. "We should probably finish eating and give Anne time to get changed."

"This Nina is the forger who will create my documentation?"

"Yes. I was put into contact with her originally while doing research for a book. We've kept as close to the truth as possible. But if Gabe sees her, he'll know something's up, and I think he may already be suspicious."

"I think they all are," said Rachel. "Holmes cautioned me about not being forthcoming with things that might put me in danger or trouble with the law. Nothing specific, but more a general warning."

Before Anne could follow up, there was another knock on the door. Anne picked up the clothing Rachel had brought with her and went into the other room to dress. There was a freedom in what women wore today. Pants—what a glorious invention. They were so much lighter and less cumbersome than all the skirts, and shifts, and petticoats and corsets. She could move freely and breathe. When she returned, she was introduced to Nina Oletta, the master forger. It was hard to reconcile the depth of skill she was purported to have with her appearance. She was a small, pixie-like woman with short black hair, an olive complexion and keen, dark eyes.

"I'm told you need new identification," Nina said, getting right down to business.

"Yes. I was married and my boyfriend arranged to have me killed," lied Anne smoothly. "I was able to get away from him but when I did so, I fled with only the clothes on my back and some loose gemstones and antique coins that have been in my family for years."

Nina nodded. "So, you are in need of not only identification but some kind of paperwork showing the gems and coins are yours and not stolen. The identification is easy enough, and I could have it by the end of tomorrow. The other paperwork will take some doing and might take a week or ten days."

"I had a feeling that my boyfriend might do something, so I hid some of the jewels. I would like to retrieve those as well so that I might get some kind of paperwork on them."

Sage leaned in. "Will you need pictures of everything, Nina? We can photograph what Anne has with her now and either bring the rest to you in the next day or two, or we can email them to you."

"Why don't I get the pictures I need for the identification and start to work on that? Then if you can get me pictures and descriptions of the gems and another list of the coins, I will work on getting all of the provenance put together."

"That sounds like a plan," agreed Sage.

"I need a plain white wall for the ID pictures. I assume you want a passport and driver's license?"

"No driver's license, but a passport, birth certificate and national health card," said Saoirse.

They posed Anne in front of the door to the bath and Nina took the pictures she needed. Anne gave her the requisite information including her birthdate, which they gave as May 19th thirty-two years ago, along with a place of birth.

"I am assuming the month and day are made up?" asked Nina with a smile.

"Yes…"

"Good. I'll find some place that's had all its records destroyed in the last thirty to thirty-five years and we'll use that. That way, there will be no record to check against." Nina reached out to take Anne's hand. "Don't worry. We've got this. When I'm done, he'll never be able to trace you. I would, however, hold off on credit cards at least for a while and stay in the larger cities. It's easier to hide in plain sight than it is in a small town or village."

"Thank you. I am most appreciative," said Anne.

"Think nothing of it. I am happy to help. So, what's up next?" asked Nina.

"Shopping and a makeover," laughed Sage.

Nina shook her head. "You are all having entirely too much fun, and if I didn't need to get on this as well as a project for another client, I'd invite myself along. Take care. *Ciao!*"

Once Nina had departed, Anne turned to the others, intrigued. "Shopping I understand, but a makeover?"

"Yes, we'll show you how to apply makeup correctly, get you some new clothes…"

"I doubt that the money I have will cover something like that."

"Not to worry. You can pay us back," said Rachel. "And I have an idea about a place for you to stay. When Holmes and I got together, I moved in with him. I have a flat in Charing Cross. It's got great access to public transportation and lots of cafes, pubs, and other places to eat and shop. It's small but it would be perfect for you. I paid for it in cash, so once we get you established, you would only have to pay for utilities—that's electricity, water, and heat."

"I would feel as though I was imposing."

"No, Anne. I'd like to do it for you."

"Anne needs to get into the Ministry of Defence building," said Saoirse. "Specifically, into Wolsey's wine cellar to access a hidden cache of gems. Think you could pull that off?"

Rachel nodded. "Yes. I have excellent contacts there and can just tell them the only time I have for a private tour is after-hours. There will be security people in there, but I can probably get them to let us in."

"All four of us?" asked Sage.

"It might have to be just you and me," admitted Rachel. She turned to Anne. "Would you be willing to trust us with the location?"

Anne nodded. "How could I not? You three ladies have done more for me at risk to yourselves than anyone in my life before." A small shiver passed through her body as she remembered the dire warning from the Warder from the night before. "I want all three of you to know how very grateful I am not only for your assistance, but your friendship. If something should happen to me..."

"What are you worried about happening?" asked Rachel.

"Nothing specific, but I have to admit that Azrael tried to prevent me from breaking through the Veil. That is the reason that boy frightened me last evening."

"I wondered about that. But you were so kind to him."

Anne smiled. "I think when I screamed, I scared him half to death."

"Well, come on, Eliza Doolittle, we have work to do," said Sage happily.

"Who?" asked Anne.

"She's a character in a play. She's a flower girl, a kind of street urchin who's taken in and made over into a lady, which of course you already are. But your speech is kind of stilted and formal," replied Sage.

"She doesn't use contractions," said Rachel. "I kept trying to think of what it was about her speech that was throwing me."

"I was going to write a historical romance, and I realized how different the language was. Our ancestors didn't start using contractions until the first part of the seventeenth century."

"What is a contraction?" Anne wondered aloud.

"A kind of shortening of words. For instance, you just said 'what is a contraction.' One of us most likely would say 'what's a contraction.' You would say "I would not think of that.' We would say 'I wouldn't think of that.'"

"I had not…"

"Hadn't."

Anne grinned. "I hadn't noticed."

"All right. Let's go hit some vintage shops. I think I know how we can dress Anne so she blends in but has a sense of her own style and is comfortable," said Sage. "Oh my god, Roark would be so pleased to hear me say that."

"Why?" asked Anne.

"Because before I met him, I worked with a woman who tried to kill me, but she did teach me to dress. It's taken the better part of a year for me to develop my own style, and I know Holmes wants Rachel to lose the frumpy look."

"I haven't bought anything frumpy since we've been together, and he's ever so grateful to you two for decimating my wardrobe," Rachel added. She turned to Anne. "It really was dreadful."

Anne mused on the idea of what sort of clothing she might enjoy having. "I like the things I have seen Saoirse wear."

"Bohemian chic, it is," said Saoirse. "Let me call Felix and see if he can't get us a driver. That would make things so much easier."

"Yes, we'll need to get Anne passes for the trains and the tube."

"What is…"

"What's," Sage corrected.

"Yes. What's the tube?"

"Oh, this one will blow your mind—that means it will confound and I think delight you. It's a kind of tunnel for a fast-moving train, which is something you won't know either, but it moves about under the city so you can avoid traffic."

Anne shook her head. "What wonderful things you have. What is the tall red vehicle that moves about the city? I saw several of them."

"Those are double decker buses. I'll tell you what, let's spend today with a driver and then once we get you settled at my flat—you are going to stay there, aren't you?" Anne nodded. "Good. Saoirse, would you mind staying there with her at least for a little while? The couch pulls out into a really comfy bed."

"I'd love to, if Anne doesn't mind the company."

"No. One of my downfalls, I think, was pride. I will take all the help I can get and be glad of it."

"Good. I think the two of you should have dinner with Gabriel and Felix tonight and stay here, and then tomorrow we'll head over to my old… rather, Anne's new flat and get her moved in."

Anne could feel tears trickling down her cheeks. Who were these amazing women who had taken her into their hearts? Was she endangering them by not telling them what the Warder had said?

"Anne, what's wrong?" said Sage, putting her arm around her.

"I am so very grateful. I do not…"

"Don't," teased Sage.

Anne wiped away the tears. "I don't know how I will ever repay you."

"Are you kidding?" quipped Sage. "I live for this kind of shit."

CHAPTER 12

elix was able to arrange for a car and
driver to be at their disposal all day. As
he closed the door after having tucked the women
into the car, he said to the driver, "Have them back by
six. We have reservations at the Grill at seven-thirty."

The driver tipped his hat and got into the car.
"Where to first, ladies?"

"Let's start from the skin out and hit makeup last.
Rigby & Peller in Mayfair," said Rachel, who was the
only one of the three who actually liked shopping for
clothes.

"On Conduit Street?" asked the driver.

"That's the one."

Once they arrived, Rachel hustled all three
women into the store, where she was greeted by the
manager like a long-lost friend. Although her clothes
might have been frumpy in the past, her lingerie had

always been decadent and risqué. They spent a little more than two hours picking up a whole new set of lingerie for Anne and several items each for Sage and Saoirse. The quality and quantity from which to choose seemed endless.

Anne was enjoying herself and finding that Rachel, like herself, loved to touch the delicate things, savoring their soft, silky feel. She was amazed at all of the choices and how each kind of bra, exhibited her bust in a different way. It did occur to her, however, that a corset did show off a woman's figure to its best advantage.

They grabbed food from several street vendors for themselves and their driver and found a place they could eat in one of the parks. Anne selected a large, salted bow-like piece of bread called a pretzel. It was warm and squishy, and she loved the difference in textures. In addition, Sage had encouraged her to try a burrito—a kind of thin, flat bread filled with meat, cheese, rice and something call beans. Both were delicious.

"I was surprised that you didn't buy many panties. I'm sure Gabe will appreciate that," teased Sage.

"You are terrible. But we did not… didn't generally wear any kind of garment down there unless your courses were upon you. Although, the ones I bought are so pretty and soft. That's one thing I keep finding myself surprised by—how very soft things are." Anne looked around and lowered her voice. "What does one do about her courses?"

"You have several options. We can go over them when we get to the flat unless…"

"I don't even know if I will have them here. I didn't in the Void. But then, I didn't feel pain or temperature or anything. When I first felt the sun on my face again, it was marvelous."

"It's interesting that you use the word 'marvelous.' Do you know that when they told your daughter she was queen, she quoted Psalm 118 and said it was 'the Lord's doing, and it is marvelous in our eyes.' I think if she knew where you were today, she'd think that was marvelous as well."

"I was so worried for her when that evil bitch, Mary, had her put in the Tower. I worried for her all through her reign. And it was a glorious reign," said Anne.

"That it was," said Rachel. "In fact, she has sometimes been referred to as 'Gloriana.' Okay, enough of the history lesson. It's back to shopping. Next up, one of my favorite vintage stores."

They collected the driver and had him take them in and around the city visiting several vintage clothing stores. By day's end, Anne had amassed an amazing collection of makeup, clothing, shoes and accessories —at least enough to see her through for a while.

By the time they got back to the Savoy, they barely had enough time to get ready for what Saoirse had called their 'double date.' Saoirse got ready first and Anne took her time, ensuring she looked like she belonged in this century. She chose to wear her favorite thing she had purchased, something Sage had called 'the perfect little black dress.'

All three of her friends had assured her that it was appropriate for their evening out. It had an off-the-shoulder neckline with a figure-hugging, elongated bodice that dropped to a ruffle which began just below the knee in front and dropped down to mid-calf in the back. She paired it with what the girls had called 'kitten heels' which seemed an odd term as to her knowledge, cats did not even wear shoes. After styling her hair, she completed the outfit with a simple set of sterling silver, drop earrings.

"Wow," said Saoirse when she walked out of the bedroom. "You are going to knock his socks off."

"It is…"

"It's," corrected Saoirse.

Anne had been working on using contractions all day and had encouraged her friends to help her with corrections, when it was just the four of them.

"It's just dinner," Anne reminded her.

"Yeah, but Gabe is no fool. My guess is you wouldn't have been so keen on that dress if you hadn't known we were meeting Gabe and Felix for dinner."

"Rachel seemed to indicate you had feelings for Felix. Does he know you're a witch?"

"He does indeed. That's no longer something they

burn you at the stake or strangle you for. Remember, I helped Rachel and Holmes send the Ripper to Hell, with the aid of the banshees."

"I always knew they were given a bad reputation by men," Anne teased.

"They certainly helped us out."

"If he doesn't—I got one right!—mind that you are... damn... you're a witch, why are you not letting him court you?"

"I suppose I could pursue Felix if I wanted, but I get mixed signals from him. Sometimes I think he's interested, and sometimes I fear that it's just my imagination. He's not like Gabe. Gabe is all in. Rachel says he's a Dom at Baker Street. I think Felix is too, but he's a gentler kind of Dom."

"Well, he seems very good at his job. And he certainly seems interested in spending time with you. He seemed rather crestfallen when we told him we were moving to Rachel's."

Before Saoirse could reply, there was a knock on the door. Saoirse opened it to admit Rachel and Sage.

Excited to see the two women, Anne asked eagerly, "Do you think we can get into the wine cellar tomorrow night?"

"I fear there's been a change in plans," said Rachel. "My friend can get me in tonight. I can go with Sage, or I can bring Sage and both of you as well. I told her Sage was doing research for a book and I needed to familiarize myself with the room for a future tour. I said I had two other friends who might be with us. So, I can say you opted out or you can come along."

A bit disappointed at the thought of missing dinner with Gabe, Anne knew she had to be practical. Too much rode on her choices right now for her to falter. "I have to go," she said. "I think I'll be able to find it more quickly than you will, especially if they've moved things around."

"Unfortunately, I agree," Saoirse said. "Anne, why don't you change, and I'll go down and break the news to the boys"

"I think you'd best tell Gabe that Anne overdid it today," Sage suggested. "While you're talking to Gabe and Felix, we'll slip down the back way. Roark was meeting with Holmes this afternoon to go over a case that has come under Scotland Yard's purview with one of Roark's clients. The client refused to sit down with the Yard unless Roark was there."

Saoirse nodded. "You go on ahead. If I can catch up with you before you meet your friend out front, I will. Otherwise, I'll wait here."

"Why don't you have dinner with Felix and Gabe? That way, Gabe won't be tempted to slip up here to offer Anne his comforting embrace."

"I could always just tell him she has menstrual cramps. That usually sends them running in the other direction," Saoirse said with a laugh.

Rachel and Sage eyed each other. "That might

not be as effective as you think. If he's been hanging out with Roark and Holmes, they may have dispelled him of any notions in that regard."

"TMI! TMI! TMI!" said Saoirse as she left the room.

"TMI?" queried Anne.

"An abbreviated slang term for too much information. Holmes doesn't mind if I'm on my period—what you called courses—as long as I'm not in pain," said Rachel.

"Men no longer think it's unclean?"

"Some do; the enlightened ones don't," said Sage.

"This isn't good," remarked Gabe to Felix as they stood waiting in the foyer where they could keep an eye on the bank of elevators. "Do you think I should have bought her flowers? Maybe we should have gone up to get them."

Felix chuckled. "I don't think I've ever seen you flustered before where a woman is concerned."

"She's different," Gabe confessed and then smiled as Saoirse stepped out of the elevator.

She was dressed in a black leather corset and trousers, over which she'd worn a black and red lace swing jacket. She had on black kitten heels, simple silver hoop earrings and a flat, heavy silver chain that ended just above her cleavage.

"Don't look now, buddy, but Saoirse looks dressed to kill."

Felix followed his line of sight and gasped. "She does indeed. Does she know you're interested in Anne?"

Gabe chuckled; Felix could be so obtuse when he tried. "I don't think she cares. She didn't put that outfit on for me. But the problem is, it's just her. Where the hell is Anne?"

Saoirse joined them right outside the door to the Savoy Grill.

"She's not coming, is she?" asked Gabe.

"No, I'm afraid not. While we were out, she got cramps, so we finished up and came back to the hotel. She was going to try and push through, but I assured her you wouldn't want her to do that."

"Of course not," said Gabe. "Why don't you two have dinner on me? I'll take Anne a heating pad and see if she needs anything else."

"Sage and Rachel are taking care of her, so she'll be fine," said Saoirse quickly—perhaps a little too quickly. "Come on Gabe, you should join us—I'll even let you pump me for information about Anne."

Gabe laughed. "And you might even tell me the truth."

"Maybe, but don't count on it."

Gabe shook his finger at her. "You are a very naughty witch. Somebody ought to jerk a knot in your pretty little tail and make you behave."

"Probably, but I don't see anyone stepping up to the plate. I'm not sure that would work on Anne. She's kind of over the whole domineering, alpha male thing."

"Not all Dominants are alpha males," said Felix. "And few true Doms are domineering. Besides, in a D/s relationship it is consensual on both sides of the slash."

"Interesting," said Saoirse, linking her arms through both men's. "How about you boys take me to dinner and tell me all about it?"

"Are you truly interested?" asked Felix, "Or just trying to be polite?"

"Felix, sweetie, haven't you figured it out yet? I rarely do anything just to be polite."

Both men laughed and headed into the restaurant, letting the maître d' know it would only be three.

Anne changed quickly into a pair of jeans and a slouchy sweater with a deep V-neck, tucking the jeans into a pair of vintage hunting boots. Then she waited with Sage and Rachel until enough time had elapsed that they could be sure Saoirse had time to get both Gabe and Felix into the restaurant. When they felt it was safe to make their exit, they headed out, utilizing the back stairs and delivery entrance.

Once outside, they hailed a cab and were dropped

a block from the Ministry of Defence building, with its imposing façade. Even in the shadows of the evening's darkness it was impressive with its stark white color and stately architecture. They moved from the front entrance where the driver had let them out around to the more discreet employee entrance where they could meet Rachel's friend.

"Linda, thanks for doing this. Sage is doing research for a book, and I need to get a couple of things straight in my head. I didn't think it would be tonight, so as we had plans with Anne, she just tagged along—if that's okay."

"No problem. I've got another forty-five minutes of work to do, and then you'll have to leave with me. Richard, the security guard, asked that you leave all your handbags and such with him."

"That's not a problem. Sage just has a notebook, and Anne didn't bring anything."

They had anticipated this and had secreted small velvet jewelry bags in their bras and had ensured their choice of clothing would hide it. Linda led them in, and they passed through a metal detector. They hadn't anticipated that, although nothing they had with them right now would set it off. Any coins they retrieved might set it off, but likely they wouldn't have to walk through the metal detector when leaving.

Once inside, Rachel handed over her large Coach hobo bag, and Linda took them down into the cellar.

"Forty-five minutes," Linda reminded them.

"It shouldn't take any longer than that. If we get through beforehand…"

"Get in the elevator. Without a key card, it will only take you to the lobby."

"Sounds good." As soon as Linda left them, Rachel turned to Anne.

"It's amazing. It's almost as if we've turned back the hands of time," she whispered. "If I close my eyes, I can almost hear Wolsey or Henry's footsteps."

Anne walked the length of the cellar, trailing her hand along the stone. In its time, the masons had been considered the best at evening out the massive blocks. But now, after being surrounded by the luxury of the Savoy, the bumpy surface and imperfections were all too apparent. She turned with deliberation, squinting her eyes and looking toward the back wall. The casks and their holders had been rearranged. She located the elaborate cask cradle she remembered but was fairly certain it wasn't in the same place where she had last seen it.

She continued to walk the floor until she reached the spot she was searching for. "Here," she said quietly. "This used to be where Wolsey, and then Henry, kept the malmsey wine. That fancy holder used to sit here." She sank down to her knees. "There was a loose brick underneath it. It'll be easier now that there isn't a cask of wine sitting on top of it." Anne felt all around and when her fingers found the almost imperceptible difference in how the brick was set into the floor, she grinned at them, gripping, then pulling up the brick to reveal a concealed compartment.

"Now, if Madge didn't play me false," she said, reaching inside and gasping as her fingers wrapped around the small box, removing it from its hiding place.

Rachel and Sage handed her their soft bags, and Anne divided the contents of the secret cache between them.

"Holy shit, Anne. There must be a fortune in there."

She grinned. "It was a small one then. I suspect it will be worth a great deal more now."

Anne placed the lid back on the now empty box, put it back where it had been, and tapped the brick back in place.

"Remind me to say a prayer for my cousin Madge," said Anne.

"I was kind of hoping your B necklace might be in there."

"The one in the painting?" asked Anne. Rachel nodded. "Artistic license. He gave me brown hair and dressed me in black. Catherine of Aragon dressed in black. I preferred jewel tones and obviously I have black hair. Same thing with the necklace—the damn thing never existed."

"Seriously?" asked Rachel with awe. "People have been searching for that thing and spinning all kinds of conspiracies since shortly after you were executed."

"I know," Anne said with genuine amusement. "I've watched them search for hundreds of years. Idiots. Even if it had existed, Henry would have had it melted down and redone for the vapid Seymour bitch. People think Catherine Howard was stupid. Not true. She was a fool, but never stupid. Jane, on the other hand, could barely put a coherent sentence together and was a papist to boot. All because Henry had to have a son. I hope the bastard knows it was my Elizabeth who was the best he sired. The other two were religious zealots."

The three women secured their jewels and headed to the elevator. They were waiting in the lobby when Linda appeared.

"Oh good. I was a little early."

"Yes, both Sage and I have been here before and just needed to confirm a few things. We're going to a pub to get fish and chips. Do you want to join us?"

"No, thanks. I'd better get home. My hubby's holding dinner."

"Thanks again, Linda. I owe you one."

"No. Just take it off the ones I owe you."

They watched as Linda headed down the street in the opposite direction they were going.

"Do you think going for fish and chips is the best idea?" asked Sage.

"What are fish and chips? I mean, I know what

fish is, but what are chips?" asked Anne.

"They're lovely pieces of fried potato," answered Sage.

"Sage? Potatoes didn't hit England until about 1588. Anne, I think you had some this morning with Saoirse. Small, golden-brown squares that are usually served alongside eggs. Do you remember?"

"Yes, we had some kind of delicious thing that was crispy on the outside and pillowy soft on the inside. They were delicious."

Rachel nodded as they walked toward the curb. "Chips are even better. But we're probably better off going back to the hotel than risking a pub tonight with the jewels on our person. We wouldn't want to lose them. Or risk being robbed."

They hailed another cab and arrived at the Savoy's back entrance in no time at all. Sneaking inside, they slipped into an elevator without being seen. Anne collected the bags full of gems from Rachel and Sage, added them to her own and gave them to Rachel, who put them in her large bag. She'd agreed to put them in her safe at the home she shared with Holmes. They were laughing and talking about what they would order for dinner when they opened the door.

"Good evening, ladies," said Gabriel, who stood in the middle of the room, his arms folded across his chest and flanked on either side by Holmes and Roark.

CHAPTER 13

Saoirse had been tense at dinner, which didn't make sense to Gabe. If Anne was truly not feeling well and Sage and Rachel were taking care of her, she should have welcomed the opportunity to have dinner alone with Felix. Instead, she had insisted he join them. When she tried to delay his leaving them to have dinner alone, Gabe's bullshit detector switched on.

"Exactly what is it you don't want me to find out upstairs?" he said without preamble.

"What? I'm not sure I know what you mean," answered Saoirse.

"The hell you don't. What are Rachel, Sage and Anne up to?"

"Gabriel, you have no reason to think that Saoirse has been less than truthful," said Felix, defending her without question.

The guy was going to have to get a grip. Saoirse was not the sweet wild child Felix believed her to be. Oh, she had that side, and Gabe liked her a lot. But he'd bet every dime he had that Saoirse was a brat of the first order. Sure, she could be sweet as honey when it suited her and probably was to those women she considered friends. But he was pretty damn sure she could also turn into the bitch goddess from Hell if she had a mind to, and especially if her target was a man.

Gabe had no doubt Felix could handle her. In fact, Gabe rather thought Saoirse was attracted to Felix but wasn't pursuing it, as the head concierge kept giving her mixed signals. Gabe also thought when push finally came to shove, Saoirse would find the gentleman Dom was more than a match for some of her more notorious behavior. He actually hoped some of it went down at the club as it would be fun to watch.

Granted, he'd probably have to keep hold of Anne to keep the tempestuous beauty from trying to take a chunk out of Felix. He got the distinct impression that even though Anne came across as a true lady, if she had to, she could get down and dirty. The image of her in that next to nothing nightgown passed before his eyes. Anne was a bit of a cock tease; he'd get that dealt with first thing.

"So, Saoirse, what are they up to?" he pressed.

"I'm pleading the Fifth."

"They don't have the Fifth Amendment here in Britain."

"Nothing is going on, Gabe."

"All right. Then you stay here with Felix, and I'll go take the girls some chocolates. Women crave chocolate when they're on their period, right?"

"Some women like salt," said Saoirse.

"Fine. I'll take her some potato chips as well."

"Why don't I just call up to check on them?" she offered.

"Felix, why don't you take Saoirse into my office and keep her there until I give you the all-clear?"

"Do you really think there's trouble?" he asked, his fingers closing around Saoirse's wrist, holding her gently in place.

"Trouble, as in they'll get themselves hurt? Doubtful. Trouble, as in doing something they shouldn't be? I'll bet you lunch on that one."

He watched as Felix looked Saoirse over and made a decision. It seemed his friend had finally decided to open his eyes about the beautiful Irish witch. Felix stood and helped Saoirse to her feet.

"I don't think I'd win that bet. Would I, Saoirse?" She said nothing. "That's what I thought. Saoirse and I will wait in your office for your call."

Saoirse seemed shocked by the change that had come over Felix. Gabe doubted she'd ever thought of him as a dominant male, but Gabe knew the truth. Saoirse's face flushed, and her pupils dilated in aroused response to this side of Felix she hadn't known existed before. Gabe grinned—he was beginning to wonder if not only they didn't know how they felt about each but how the other felt about them. Saoirse didn't play at Baker Street, but if she was as attracted to Felix as Gabe suspected, she had some things to learn about him. Felix was very popular and knew how to deal with a woman who needed a firm hand. Anne and her compatriots might well have done their good friend Saoirse a favor by giving her a chance to see the man in all his gentleman Dom glory.

As Felix headed with the witch toward the offices, Gabe walked toward the elevators. He was just about to place a call on his cell to Roark and Holmes when the two entered the hotel.

"I thought you would be romancing the lovely Lady Anne," said Holmes.

"Hmm, doesn't look like she slapped him," said Roark.

Ignoring the banter, Gabe got right to the point. "Do either of you know where Sage and Rachel are?"

Holmes raised an eyebrow in surprise. "Rachel said she'd hang out with Sage until Roark and I got back from Scotland Yard. We actually broke the guy's alibi fairly quickly and once we did that, he caved and confessed."

"Yes," agreed Roark. "I was going to go get the

girls, and Holmes was coming in to see if we could join you for dessert. Is there a problem?"

"Did I just see Felix with Saoirse?" asked Holmes.

"Yes, he's taking her to my office. I think if they were further along their journey, Saoirse might well be receiving a dose of discipline from Felix. It might be amusing if it weren't for the fact that I am pretty damn sure I'm being lied to.

Anne begged off, or rather had Saoirse beg off, pleading cramps. Supposedly, Sage and Rachel were going to take her a heating pad and look after her. The more I thought about it and watched Saoirse, the more I knew I wasn't getting the whole story. So as the book always says, Holmes, I do believe '*the game is afoot.*' What do you say we go up to Anne and Saoirse's room and see what's what?"

"You don't think they'll be there, do you?" Roark said, shaking his head.

"Good lord, what do you think they're up to?" asked Holmes.

"I have no idea, but I think we'd best find out, don't you?"

Holmes and Gabriel got off on the floor where Saoirse and Anne's room was located. Roark continued up to the floor where his and Sage's suite was, saying he'd join them as soon as he ensured they weren't there.

Gabe knocked on the door, and when there was no answer, used his master code to let himself into the room, calling for Anne just in case she was in the bedroom. Not only was no one there, but it appeared the room had been empty for the past couple of hours. None of the lights in either room were on, and when he felt the lightbulbs they were cool to the touch. There was a soft knock on the door and Holmes opened it to allow Roark to join them.

"Sage hasn't been in our room for some time. Is it just me, or is there something off about Anne Hastings?"

"Off? How?" asked Holmes.

Gabe nodded. "I said the same thing to Felix this afternoon. Not that she's a bad person, but there's something not quite right that I can't put my finger on."

"I know when interrogating three suspects, the first thing you do is separate them so they can't coordinate their stories," offered Holmes, taking a seat.

"Roark can take Sage upstairs to their suite. I'll tell Felix he may want to settle into my office, and you can use this room."

"What about you and Anne? And I take it there is a you and Anne," said Holmes with a sly grin.

Gabe returned the grin with a predatory smile of his own. "She might not know it yet, but there is definitely a me and Anne. The caveman in me would like to just toss her over my shoulder and take her home to deal with her…"

"That's an excellent idea in general, only it might

not be a good idea for you and Anne just yet," said Holmes. "So, I will take my very beautiful wife-to-be home where I can interrogate her thoroughly, and you and Anne can stay here and…well, do what you have to do."

"That sounds good. Would you mind stopping in my office and telling Felix he might want to get Saoirse another room? We have a couple of vacancies, and I have a couple of comps I need to use up. Tell him I'll pick up the tab. What do you say we chat in the morning?" said Gabe.

"My guess is the three of them will come back here. I say we wait for them," said Roark, sitting down in one of the wingbacks. "My little minx is going to have a very sore bottom inside and out when I'm done with her. She knows better."

"So does Rachel."

"God, I envy the two of you," Gabe said as he moved restlessly around the room. "I never thought I would…"

"Would what? Envy us, or have a woman of your own?"

Gabe chuckled. "Both."

Before he could say anything else, they heard the electronic lock click open. Holmes and Roark stood, and all three men turned to face the door, crossing their arms as they waited.

"Good evening, ladies," intoned Gabriel as Sage, Rachel and Anne entered the room.

He watched with fascination as both Sage and Rachel realized they'd been found out and were most likely facing discipline from Roark and Holmes respectively. Anne, on the other hand, didn't have a clue. Rather than appearing remorseful or embarrassed, she straightened her shoulders and tilted her chin up in defiance.

"Gabriel? What are you and your two comrades doing in my room?" she asked, her tone and demeanor imperious.

"Sage," said Roark in a perfectly even tone of voice. "Upstairs now. You and I are going to have a little talk about what precisely went on this evening and where the three of you have been."

If you didn't know Roark and the loving way he normally addressed his wife, you'd never know how truly pissed off he was. But Gabe had known the man a long time, and if the tone of Roark's voice was any indication, Sage was in for a rough night.

Holmes, on the other hand, said absolutely nothing, merely strode forward, leaned down and tossed Rachel over his shoulder before walking out the door. Rachel started to say something that turned into a squeak when Holmes hand connected with her ass. Gabe guessed her night wasn't going to go much better than Sage's.

"I'll let Felix know of our plans," said Holmes. "I'll check with the two of you in the morning."

"Gabriel, I will leave Ms. Hastings in your most

capable hands," Roark said. "Sage, I believe I told you to go to our suite."

He made his way past Gabe and Anne, fisting Sage's auburn locks and leading her out of the room, closing the door behind them.

"I demand to know what you think you're doing," snarled Anne—her dark eyes flashing fire as she moved past him.

"Getting to the bottom of whatever's going on around here," he said turning to follow her movements and so that he could keep an eye on her.

"You have no right to question me."

"That's where you're wrong, Anne. I'm the head of security in this hotel. I have every right to question you if I think you are up to something nefarious."

Anne's body lost some of its rigidity. "Nefarious? I'm not familiar with that word."

That took him a bit aback. Anne was intelligent. How could she not know the meaning of the word nefarious?

"Nefarious, it means villainous, disreputable, immoral—in other words, things the Savoy doesn't want done in its hotel."

"Nefarious. An interesting word, but I can assure you nothing nefarious is being done in your hotel, Gabriel," she said dismissively, turning her back on him.

"Why don't you tell me what the three of you were doing, and I'll decide for myself."

"I don't owe you any explanation," she said, turning back to face him.

"Maybe and maybe not. But let me ask you this. Are you really going to let your friends get into trouble with their Doms on your behalf?"

"Doms? You mean Roark and Holmes? I didn't think they were going to your club."

Gabe laughed. "So, you know about Baker Street. Interesting. We can chat about that some other time. Roark, Sage, Holmes and Rachel don't play at D/s; they live it."

Anne walked past him and sat on the settee, resting her arms along the back, her body open and alluring. He wondered if she knew that he was imagining her sitting that way without her clothes on, and decided, given the smile that played across her lips, she was keenly aware of it. "You know," she mused, "I've tried asking Saoirse about it, but she says she doesn't know much."

"If she and Felix continue along the path I think they will, she'll find out soon enough. What would you like to know?"

"So, you're a Dominant?" He nodded. "What does that mean?"

"It means I like to be in control, especially in the bedroom."

"So, you just do what you want and expect the woman to lie there?"

Gabe chuckled and watched how the sound

affected her. Her skin flushed the loveliest shade of pink and he wondered if her bottom would color as easily when spanked. Her eyes widened and her breath became a little faster and shallower. She was definitely intrigued by, and not unfamiliar with, the idea, which made sense as she was friends with Sage and Rachel. "If all she does is lie there, I'm not doing it right."

"So, what does that mean? I don't understand."

"I like control," he said, enjoying where this conversation was going. "And I think there's a rhythm and flow to how things should be between couples. One needs to be dominant and the other submissive."

"I've never been subservient and will never submit to another man for as long as I live," she vowed. "No one will ever have power over me again."

The vehemence in her tone surprised him. Partly, that was his own fault. He'd probably been spending too much time at the club or around Sage and Rachel. Sometimes he forgot there were an awful lot of misconceptions around the lifestyle.

"D/s is about a power exchange," he explained. "No one has any power over anyone that isn't freely given. And I believe there's a huge difference between being subservient and submitting to the authority of your partner."

"Aren't you the least bit worried that Holmes and Roark might hurt Sage and Rachel?"

"Not in the least. Wait, that's not precisely true. If

Sage and Rachel cop an attitude with them, like you're doing with me, or if they think they're not going to offer up the entire truth, then I imagine that come morning both Sage and Rachel may have some trouble sitting down."

Anne shot straight up on her feet. "You mean your friends would beat mine?"

"Hold on. Sage and Rachel are my friends too. And no one is going to beat anyone. Do I suspect they'll both get spanked for whatever the lot of you are up to? Yes."

"Is that it, Gabriel?" she purred. "Do you want to spank me?"

Gabe wondered if in the past, pulling mercurial changes had worked for her. He guessed she had a bad habit of topping from the bottom, which wouldn't work with him. But he wondered if she did it because she'd been given no other choice. If no one had ever valued honesty and openness from her, was it her fault if it wasn't her default behavior?

Was Anne afraid? If so, of what?

"Anne, I'm going to assume you've never been involved in a D/s relationship. Do I want to spank you? You have no idea how much—partly because I think it would be a pretty quick way to get to the truth and partly because you have the most glorious ass I've ever seen. I liked the way your body looked in that next-to-nothing nightgown this morning, but I'd really love to see you with nothing on at all."

"I wouldn't mind seeing you that way…" Her tone of voiced all but dripped honey, but Gabe had no intention of getting caught in that sticky web.

He shook his head. "No, Anne. I'm the Dom. If we go forward, you'll be my sub."

As quickly as she had leaned into him, she drew back. "Never," she snarled.

Interestingly intense reaction.

"Never is a long time," he said in a soothing voice. "I want you, Anne, and not just for a night or two. I find you compelling and frustrating, and I can't remember the last time I wanted a woman without any end point laid out in a contract."

"So, you want to hurt me?" she asked, her voice raw, honest, defenseless.

Gabe was beginning to believe the haughty, regal act was just that, and the haunting vulnerability he heard now was the real Anne, the woman who hid beneath the armor someone had forced her to wear.

"Not really," he said gently, yet firmly. "I want to push your limits. And if we go forward, you will submit to my authority, which means if you try to lead me around by my dick or lie to me, I'll spank your ass so fast and so hard, you'll think twice before doing it again."

Where the hell was all this coming from? When had he decided he wanted something more, something special, something akin to what his friends had?

"You expect me to just give over my life to you?

To trust you?" He could feel her walls coming back up. "Based on what? One day of knowing you?"

He'd been leaning forward and now sat back. She didn't need to feel threatened or attacked. "I think time is irrelevant. Sometimes you just know, and how much time is involved doesn't matter. I think you feel the same pull to me that I feel to you."

"I'm sure it has not escaped your notice that I'm attracted to you," she admitted, her body beginning to relax.

His painfully hard cock was really glad to hear that and see her body losing its rigidity.

"We don't have to rush into anything," he said, "but you have to know that any relationship with me is going to involve D/s. It's part and parcel of who I am at my core. I need to have control. You will have to submit to me, to my authority, but there are proto-cols in place."

"What kind?"

Her mercurial changes were going to give him whiplash. This was not the discussion he'd been planning to have with her, and he wondered briefly if she was subtly keeping him away from what he wanted to know. Well, two could play at that game. No. She wasn't a suspect. Anne was someone he cared about —someone he was fast falling in love with.

CHAPTER 14

*J*n her entire life, Anne had never wanted anything as much as she wanted this man. She ached for him in a way she had scoffed at when others described it. Henry had been her only lover, despite what had been whispered about her. And she hadn't given herself to Henry; he'd taken what he wanted. Her virginity had been lost in a fit of temper, and twice he had impregnated her when he forced her to have sex with him. Elizabeth had been conceived on a night when he had been both gentle and virile. It had been the first time she had climaxed, and one of the only times. Henry had not cared for her pleasure, only his own.

So, it shouldn't be that surprising that Gabe filled her with desire. She'd already climaxed once, just dreaming about him. His words drew her back to the present, and the evening of pleasure he was offering her.

"We can start with the stoplight system," Gabe explained. "Green for everything is fine. Yellow for you need to slow down or take a break. Red for stop."

"But only up to a point."

Gabe shook his head. "No. You say red, and everything stops. We can talk it out or you can walk away."

"But not if I'm being punished."

"Nope, even then."

"And in exchange for allowing you to have control and discipline me whenever you feel like it…"

"Again, no. If we enter into this, there will be rules and you'll know them. You won't ever be disciplined without knowing why. My guess is you'll do whatever it is—like prevaricating with me right now—knowing full well, I'm going to spank you."

"And what do I get out of this submission?"

"The quick, easy answer is multiple orgasms."

Anne laughed, but joined him on the settee. Gabe continued his train of thought, determined to persuade her to submit to him.

"The more complicated response is that you get me and my protection, my caring, my everything. If you need something, I want you to turn to me and allow me to take care of it for you. It makes me feel good to be able to do that. It gives me purpose. Most subs find a certain peace in their submission. And not all subs are submissive to all Doms. I doubt you could pull that off. In a club, I'd expect you to be polite, and the same with our friends. But if some asshole tells you to drop to your knees…" he said snapping his fingers and pointing to the ground.

"I can punch him?"

Gabe grinned. "No, you call me, and I'll drop him to *his* knees."

"I think I'd rather like that," she said, crawling toward him on the settee.

Anne was having trouble breathing steadily. Her nipples were as hard as the gemstones wrapped around her neck. She could feel desire swirling in her nether region and her skin felt like it was on fire—not in a bad way, but as if Gabriel held a fiery torch to her arousal, threatening to ignite it and let it burn out of control. Why did his very words make her feel more longing than she'd ever felt in Henry's arms? She brought her mouth down on his, leaning into him and allowing his body to cradle hers. There was such strength and comfort as she lay on his body, his hard cock pulsing beneath her.

"I meant what I said, Anne," he said holding her back. "If we get involved, I'm the Dom and you're the sub."

God, he was a persistent bastard.

"Why don't you just shut up and kiss me? We'll figure the rest out later."

"No. That's what they do in vanilla relationships

and get all screwed up. I need you to understand how it's going to be, and I need you to consent to it. Once you have, we'll start in the same way we'll go on."

"What do you mean by vanilla?"

"A non-D/s relationship."

"Ah," she said, smiling. "Green. I am most definitely green."

"Not good enough. I need you to tell me you want to submit to me, that you want me to be your Dom."

"You're awfully—what did Rachel call Holmes? Ah yes, bossy."

"Yes, I am."

"And if I agree, you're going to spank me?"

"Not if you answer me truthfully. But if you lie to me or try to evade my questions, then I will put you over my knee and spank you and not in a fun way."

"Is there a fun way?"

He chuckled. The sound floated across her body as if he were dragging a silk scarf all along her flesh.

"Most definitely. That's the first rule. You don't lie to me."

"When do I get these multiple orgasms?" she asked provocatively.

Gabe chuckled. "Every single time I fuck you. And trust me, you'll get fucked at least a couple of times a day. The best way to re-establish positive feelings and put our relationship back on track is for me to fuck you after you're punished. That way you'll know for certain you've been forgiven."

"Then let's begin," she purred.

"Fine. Discipline is always done with you naked."

"You don't know that I'm not going to tell you the honest truth."

"Don't I?"

"I think you just want to see me naked."

"I'd be lying to you if I said I didn't. Naked, Anne. If you can't submit to that…"

"Fine," she snapped, trying to sit up.

Gabe's hand cracked down on her jean-clad rump. Anne was surprised at the amount of sting and heat that radiated from that single blow through the thick denim.

"Second rule—sass me or give me attitude, especially when you're in trouble with me, and you get spanked. For the record, you're in trouble with me."

"Gabriel," she said. As he shook his head, she continued, "What?"

"When we're alone or you're in trouble, it's Sir or Master."

"I will never call you or any other man Master."

"I don't give a damn what you call any other man, and I can wait until I've earned that title in your mind."

Anne stood up and Gabriel moved from the settee to one of the chairs across from it, lounging like a great lion ready to rip into its prey. Well, she would show him she was no little gazelle. Lust bloomed within her, and she closed her eyes to revel in it. She pulled the sweater over her head, smiling when Gabe groaned as he stared at her breasts. The bra she had on provided as much support as a corset but was much more comfortable. She reached back and unhooked the bra then let it drop to the floor.

"You'll have to help me with my boots," she said, placing her heel on the edge of the chair between his spread legs.

"Careful."

"Trust me, I intend to be very careful not to injure that."

He chuckled and pulled off first one boot and then the other, his fingers lingering on her skin. As she shimmied out of the jeans, the air in the room washed over her naked flesh. Her nipples had been hard from the moment she'd stepped into the room and had only grown stiffer as they talked.

"God, you're gorgeous. From this point forward, your body belongs to me, every little bit of it."

"And what about yours?" she asked, starting to wonder if this was such a good idea.

"Everything I am and have is yours. Come closer," he said, his voice deep and heavy with lust. She stepped up to where he sat waiting for her, both of them breathing a little harder with desire.

Gabe reached up for her breast, cupping it, his hand closing around it gently before gliding over her skin. Anne moaned. This was so much better than her own hand. The pleasure was so intense, her knees almost buckled. Gabe traced her dusky areolas, staring as impossibly they tightened even more. He strummed his thumb across them, provoking another moan.

"Please, Gabe," she said huskily, until his thumb and forefinger closed on her nipple and pinched, hard.

"What did I say you were to call me?"

"Sir… Please, Sir."

"That's a good girl," he crooned seductively.

God, if he didn't get on with it, she was going to come right here where she stood. She could feel her entire body alight with need and arousal. Her pussy was softening, readying itself to sheathe his hard cock.

"Where were you tonight?" he asked softly.

"We just decided to go out."

"That's the first lie. Well, I suppose technically the second as the first was the one you had Saoirse tell me, but I probably shouldn't count that one. For each lie, I'm going to spank your ass five times. Do you understand?"

"Yes, Gabriel, bu…" What she was about to say ended in a gasp, as he pinched her nipple a second time. "Yes, Sir."

"Better. I'm going to have to go shopping and find some nipple clamps for you. You have such sensitive, responsive tits. And your skin. We may have to do some wax play. Where were you?"

He was keeping her so unbalanced, it was difficult

to come up with a convincing lie. And she had no way of knowing what any of the other girls would say…. Gabe pinched the first nipple again, harder this time.

"Take too long, and I'll know you're thinking of lying to me. Next time you do, I'll pinch your clit and you'll get another five. It would be a shame to have to punish that sweet little jewel before I get to pleasure it. Where were you, Anne?"

This really wasn't fair. If she wanted to keep him in the dark, she needed to be able to think, which was becoming increasingly difficult to do. He had the most amazing hands and she'd been too close to him far too often not to know that he had a ridiculously big cock.

"I went with Rachel and Sage to a building, I don't know the name, but it was once York Place." She hated having to admit this. She had no way to know if it was similar to what her friends were saying. Her annoyance wasn't helping with the situation. Instead of feeding her anger or indignation at being treated this way, all it was doing was fueling her arousal.

Gabe nodded, seemingly unsurprised at her admission. Had he known all along where she was? If he had, had he known why? "The Ministry of Defence. Why?"

"Because Sage and Rachel wanted to see Wolsey's wine cellar."

This time the bastard reached between her legs and pinched her little love nubbin. Anne cried out.

"And that makes ten you owe me. Let me make this a bit easier. Either of them could get in there during the day. They both have connections so that means they didn't want anything on the books, which means you wanted to see it. Why?"

She knew she was taking too long. What had he said about colors? Red for complete stop, which probably meant he wasn't going to fuck her either and she wanted him to fuck her so badly. Yellow. That was it. Yellow meant she needed a break.

Just as Gabe reached for her nipple again, she said, "Yellow."

Surprisingly, he stopped. And he didn't seem angry, just respectful. "Yellow? Or red?"

"Definitely yellow. I need a moment. I don't want to stop." Anne could hear tears creeping into her voice.

"Come here, Anne," he said, guiding her between his knees and encouraging her to sit on his lap. "What do you need?"

"I suppose stopping the interrogation is out of the question?"

"No, but it means everything else stops as well," he said, placing his hand between her naked thighs and tracing the wet seam of her sex.

Anne's body arched back, and she knew if he touched her again, she would go off like fireworks.

His thumb and forefinger grasped her clit and gave it a hard tug. It wasn't as bad as a pinch but definitely backed her off the edge.

"Uh-uh. You don't come when you're being disciplined unless I tell you to, or part of your punishment is forced orgasms."

"Orgasms? Plural? You really think you can make me come more than once?"

Was that even possible? She knew that men could only come once without some kind of recovery time, but could he provide her with so much pleasure that her world would explode with vibrant colors and that wonderful feeling the French described as "*la petite mort?*" His large finger stroked down through the wet petals of her sex, making her shiver.

"Baby, as responsive as you are, that's a given. What I want is to get you so hot and bothered that when I shove my cock in, you orgasm just from that. Where are you?"

"London," she said, confused, and he laughed.

"No, on the stoplight."

"Mostly green, but still a little yellow."

"What can I do to help?"

"Why do you need to know what I was doing?"

"So, I was right. You were the reason the three of you went tonight."

"You tricked me," she accused.

"I did, but honestly I was pretty damn sure I was right. Want to tell me why? Or do we need to make it

fifteen you owe me? I want to remind you that this is
not the fun kind of spanking, although I suspect it'll
get you even more aroused. Since this is the first time
you're going to be spanked, I mean to make it
memorable."

"There were some jewels that have been in my
family for centuries." This was the story they had
decided upon. "I needed to get them. I left an abusive
boyfriend and when the opportunity came, I just ran.
I need the money."

"That's why you didn't have any luggage."

She nodded. "I had an opening to get away and I
took it."

"Why have Saoirse lie to me?"

"Because I didn't want you involved. I didn't
mean to lie to you. But like when I ran away, the
opportunity came up and I took it. I never meant to
start a relationship with you. I wanted to fuck you, but
I didn't think it would mean anything."

"And now?" he asked softly.

She softened, looking at him with an odd mixture
of regret, reluctance and desire. "I think it means
everything."

CHAPTER 15

Gabe's arms circled around her, pulling her close, and for the first time in her life, Anne knew what it was to be comforted by a man who cared about her.

"I'm sorry, Sir," she said and knew it wasn't just words. She was genuinely sorry as she knew she'd hurt him and realized that wasn't something she wanted to do.

"Where are the gems now?"

They hadn't talked about that. In fact, they thought they'd gotten away with it. She'd been improvising so far. They'd agreed on the abusive boyfriend story, but not on the gems. Anne was scrambling in her head to come up with a plausible explanation. The sharp pinch on her nipple refocused her thinking.

"They weren't there," she said in a rush. "We

found their hiding place and the box they were in, but not the gems."

He studied her, eyes narrowed. "That's fifteen. What are your plans?"

How did he know she was lying? She sighed and admitted, "Rachel is going to let me stay in her flat until I get on my feet. It won't cost much, just utilities."

"No. In for a penny; in for a pound. You'll stay with me. Besides, I know Felix was going to ask Rachel about buying her place for himself. And after tonight with Saoirse, I rather imagine he'll want to do that sooner rather than later."

Anne bristled. He couldn't dictate to her. "You can't just decide where I'm going to live."

"I can and I did. Besides, you like Felix and Saoirse, you want them to have a nice flat, and my place is bigger. I want you with me. Say yes, Anne."

She looked into his deep ice blue eyes and saw the longing and all the feeling there. And she couldn't resist. "Yes," she agreed.

He kissed her, pressing his lips to hers. She'd been kissed before, plenty of times, but this was not that awkward fumbling that left her wanting. This wasn't a boy who didn't know how, or a king who couldn't be bothered. No, this was a man who wanted her, who wanted to pleasure her. His tongue surged past her lips, and she felt herself open for him, allowing his tongue to slide along and dance with hers.

She kissed him back. That, she'd never done. Oh, she might have started something, like she tried to with Gabe, but once the man responded, she'd always just allowed him to take over. She let her tongue follow his as it retreated, letting it glide into his mouth cautiously, growing bolder as he moaned and stroked her spine.

Anne was beginning to think she could spend eternity kissing Gabriel Watson. She loved the way his tongue slid along her bottom lip before going back in to taste her once more as his hand, between her legs, stroked her again.

"I want you," she whispered against his mouth.

"You're sitting on the evidence of how I feel," he chuckled, "but you owe me fifteen."

"Wait, what?" she said, confused.

"Look, Anne, one of the things I believe in is consistency and doing what I say I will. I want you to know you can count on that."

She pulled back, staring at him. "But we kissed. I thought you were going to make love to me."

"And I will," he assured her. "But first, you're going to put yourself over my lap, and then I'm going to spank you for lying and playing games with me. Then I'll fuck you long and hard, and after we've rested, then I'll make love to you." He helped her stand. "Up you go, let's get this done."

Anne wasn't sure why, but as Gabe guided her over his lap, every nerve ending in her body suddenly came alive. She lay across his legs, his cock throbbing beneath her belly. God, if he could fuck like he could kiss, this might all be worth it. She tried to even out her breathing as he ran his hands over her ass, slowly caressing the swells and valleys. She lay there waiting, but waiting for what, she wasn't sure.

She felt a small upsurge in the air, before Gabe's hand came crashing down in a decidedly harsh smack. Anne yowled, surprised by the pain.

"That's one. This first time you don't have to count, and you can make all the noise you need to, but there's fourteen more to come, and this won't get any easier. Can you take this from me?"

Something about the situation made her want to prove herself. And of course, she still felt heat rising between her legs, and he had promised… "Yes, Sir," she said, hissing as the next blow landed.

The gentle fire that had warmed her soul earlier had become a wildfire racing across her skin as she bit back several choice swear words. She was pretty damn sure he didn't want to hear those.

"That's two."

And then there was no more talking as he laid down a series of five more additional smacks, lighting up her system, and not in the way she'd reveled in before. Tears began to well in her eyes. She didn't try to stop them, mostly because she knew she couldn't. As they fell, she realized it was such a release to cry,

letting out all of the emotion—grief, longing, rage—
that she'd felt.

Anne cried as Gabe rained hellfire down on her
sensitive flesh. Yet soon, she felt a kind of soft serenity
settling over her. She didn't try to keep count, because
she knew Gabe would give her no more, no less than
what he'd promised. This man would keep his word to
her. She was quickly learning there was a peace and
strength that came with submitting to Gabe. If she
said red, she knew it would be done, but she didn't
want it to be. She'd never been so connected to
anyone as she was to this handsome, dominant man.

But behind the peace came a surge of arousal that
rose in her system. Her pussy began to pulse in the
same rhythm as the spanking. It didn't make any
sense, but there it was. Pleasure in her punishment.
He was smacking her ass over and over, making it
tender and raw and yet she'd never been more
aroused in her entire life. It was perverse, and yet she
knew when he went to fuck her, she'd be more than
ready for him.

So much of her life had been lived in public with
prying eyes and spies everywhere, but with Gabe
disciplining her, it was only the two of them. Nothing
else mattered. In this moment, in this room with
Gabe, she could be herself. Not Thomas Boleyn's
daughter, not the whore, not the Queen of England,
not even Henry's doomed queen or Elizabeth's
mother. No, here she was just Anne.

And the man who was wailing on her ass… No, disciplining her, imposing his authority over her, with her consent… was Gabriel, her lover, her Dom.

His hand stilled, and he laid it against the hot aching globes of her backside as if he meant to hold the heat and sting in forever. He caressed her willing flesh, soothingly, lovingly.

"You all right, sweetheart?" he asked, his voice surprisingly and endearingly tender.

"Yes, Sir," she said, feeling a deeper peace than she had ever known or could have even imagined. "Green, Sir."

"Okay then, let me help you up." He steadied her as she stood, pulling her gently back into his lap. "I like to take a little time to come down. A spanking is pretty intense for me as well."

He cradled her against his chest and just let her rest against him as he rocked her back and forth. Anne could not recall a single time in her life when she had ever felt so cared for. She dozed, completely replete in his arms. It wasn't until she felt his hand slip between her legs that she came fully alert again. Responding to his touch, she moaned in pure pleasure, opening her legs to him so he could have what he wanted.

"You're so fucking wet."

She smiled. How could he make something that was dirty sound like a declaration of love?

"There will come a time when I teach you just

how I like my cock to be sucked, and I'll eat my fill of
your pussy. I'll also teach you how I want to be
greeted, but that can all wait. Just like later tonight,
I'm going to make long, slow, sweet love to you,
making you writhe beneath me because you can't
even vocalize your pleasure, but not this time. Go into
the bedroom and get up on the bed."

He helped her up and caressed her buttocks,
sending her to the bedroom. She crawled up on the
bed, wincing when her tender ass scraped along the
incredibly soft sheets and mattress. Apparently, a soft
bed and silky sheets were no match for a blistered
backside.

She could hear Gabriel moving in the other room.
The rustling of fabric and soft click of metal from his
belt buckle came to her clearly. He was getting
undressed. Would he come in wearing a nightshirt?
She'd always wanted a really good look at a man—
their bodies were so different from hers—but was
considered wanton for saying it.

Still, whatever happened next, they were going to
have sex. The idea thrilled her. The poor man had no
idea how much she wanted to have sex with him—
even more now than she had when she just thought
they were having dinner. Saoirse had told her Gabe
would most likely ask her if she was clean or healthy,
which meant free of any sexually transmitted diseases.
He would also ask her about birth control. In this new
time, women could crave sex and not worry about

getting pregnant. There was a pill she could take, but until it was completely effective, Gabe could wear something on his cock to prevent pregnancy. Saoirse had assured her it wouldn't diminish the feeling much for either of them. It relieved her to know this.

Gabe walked in as naked as she was. He seemed perfectly at home in that state. She studied his body, biting her lip. He was gorgeous, easily the most gorgeous man she'd ever seen. Henry had already been starting to layer on the fat that had become so much a part of how the world had seen him. Gabriel, gloriously, looked nothing like that. Henry had told her he was masculine perfection. He lied. Gabe was magnificent—with broad shoulders and a chest and abdomen like chiseled stone. His torso sat atop long, powerful, well-muscled thighs and his calves were a work of art.

Blonde hair dusted across his chest, with a slightly darker line leading down to the nest of curls that served as a frame for his enormous cock. It wasn't just long but had incredible girth. On his best day, Henry's hadn't been half that size. Gabe's member jutted not just straight out, but upwards, the weeping head almost touching his navel. She had never wanted to put her mouth on a man there, but with Gabriel she might make an exception to that rule.

CHAPTER 16

"**S**pread your legs for me, Anne."

She blushed so prettily at his command. Gabe studied her, enjoying what he saw. For a woman who was as responsive as she was and whose natural inclination was to be a bit on the predatory side, there was clearly also a part of her that felt unsure and even a bit shy. When she dropped the barriers and showed her vulnerability like this, it was enchanting. It made her more feral, primitive side even more alluring to him.

"I'm healthy, Anne," he assured her. "Are you on birth control?"

"I'm clean. I'm not on the pill, but I plan to get established here with a doctor."

He leaned down and kissed her. "That's all right, Anne. I can wear a condom. I have some with me."

He walked back to where his clothes were and came back, rolling the condom smoothly over his cock. Even from the side of the bed, he could smell her arousal, sweet and enticing. It made him that much harder, if that were possible. Shy now, she tried to close her legs.

"You keep them open for me. That's my pussy, and I want to see it in all its creamy glory."

"Gabe," she laughed nervously.

"Flip over, baby. On your hands and knees…"

"Gabe?"

He knew some women didn't like what they felt was one of the most male dominant positions, while others didn't like it because it seemed more impersonal. Gabe didn't care at the moment what Anne thought. For one thing, she was still being punished. And for another, this was one of his favorite positions, so she'd just have to get used to the idea. Whatever she might be thinking, her objection was only mental not physical. He knew he would bring her to orgasm without any problems. In fact, he meant to make and keep her sore for a while from how many times he fucked her in a single night.

She was so wet, he could use her natural juices to lubricate his sheathed cock. He dipped his fingers into her, drawing out the copious viscosity before slathering it over his cock, running his hand up and down its length.

When he didn't relent, she did as she was told, and he crawled up behind her. Anne had a decidedly hourglass figure, and her nipped-in waist and broad hips would make her easy to fuck. He ran his hands down her spine, pushing on her shoulders.

"Down in front."

"I don't know that I like this."

"I understand, and I know why, but I'm going to ask you to do this for me and also tell you that when you're being punished, this is the only way you'll get fucked. Green or red, Anne."

She mumbled something under her breath, and he smacked her painful ass.

"You watch your language. Next time, it'll get you spanked another five times."

"Yes, Sir," she said begrudgingly.

He nestled up behind her, perversely enjoying the way she winced as he snuggled against her very red bottom. "You have the most beautiful ass, Anne. And so much prettier in a vivid shade of crimson."

Anne giggled and buried her face in a pillow. "I'm sorry, Sir. I don't mean to be disrespectful."

"I didn't think you were."

He loomed over and behind her, gripping her hips to hold her in place. This way, he could control both depth of penetration and movement. He lined his cock up with the entrance to her core and rimmed her with it. There would come a time he would fuck her asshole, but he had a sneaky suspicion that would be a first for her. As the head of his cock breached the opening to her pussy, she moaned. He was big and didn't want to hurt her, but God, he needed to be inside her.

Slowly he began to push himself into her. Her body shook as it accepted his offering and stretched to accommodate him. She was tight and hot and the best thing he'd ever felt in his entire life.

"God, Gabriel," she sighed.

From the way she voiced it and the way she pushed back against him, he knew it was frustration and not pain. He hesitated, allowing her to adjust, savoring the way she felt physically and how she made him feel—tender, protective, vulnerable, loving—all at the same time. He pressed all the way inside her so that his groin was snug up against her ass and he was buried balls deep in her.

Gabe pulled almost all the way out before thrusting back in. She was taut as a wire and when he did it the second time, her orgasm crashed over her, and she called his name. He knew this first time, it would take every ounce of control he had not to come the moment she did. He had promised her multiple climaxes and he meant to deliver. He stilled and let her ride the crest of the wave and revel in it. Anne reached back for him, and he allowed her to connect. He'd be stricter the next time he spanked her, but this time was all about connection.

He drew back and surged in again, allowing them to find a rhythm together. Granted, he controlled the rhythm, but Anne seemed to be in sync with him in a way no woman ever had before. Gabe began to fuck her hard and rough, hammering her tight pussy and making it his own. He didn't just want her backside to hurt come tomorrow morning, but he wanted her pussy to ache from his use and for her to know he had claimed what was his.

His hips rocked back and forth, driving his cock deep before pulling almost out and slamming into her again. She tried to move in time with him, but he held her steady. He pounded into her repeatedly, relentlessly, ruthlessly and Anne screamed as she came again. Yeah, that's what he wanted. He grinned in satisfaction.

As she came down from her high, Gabe angled his body so that he could hit her G-spot again and again, and he could feel her body responding. One thing about Anne—she liked being pleasured and was learning how quickly and deeply he could make her feel.

Her hands grasped the end of the mattress as he fucked into her powerfully. Harder and harder he hammered her. The familiar tingle crept down his spine, settling at the base, and he knew he didn't have much more to give her this time.

He held her tight, grinding his groin into her punished ass as her pussy clamped down, contracting all up and down his cock, milking it as he pumped her full of his cum—well actually, the condom, but he smiled thinking what it would be like to see her filled to overflowing and the residual dribbling down the inside of her thigh.

Sated for the moment, Gabe pressed her down into the mattress, lying atop her briefly, savoring the connection between them. Then, he gently slipped off her body and pressed kisses all up and down her spine until he nuzzled her neck. She gave him a soft, pleasured moan that made him feel all too satisfied with himself.

"Stay here," he whispered, rolling off the bed and heading into the bath so he could dispose of the condom before joining her under the covers.

Once he climbed into the bed, he lay on his back, cradling her close to his side and enjoying the way she felt lying next to him, as Shakespeare had said, '*to sleep, perchance to dream.*'

Anne woke the next morning to find herself alone. Had last night been a dream?

She moved her body and groaned. No—it was no dream. Her flesh ached in places she hadn't even known it could. When Henry had first come to her bed, he would fuck her once or twice and then leave her to sleep alone. Gabriel had fucked her several more times than that—each time bringing her to orgasm multiple times, and he'd slept with her, she knew, at least until the sun started to rise. And he hadn't just shared her bed, he'd slept with her either lying on his back, cradling her against his side or spooned with her back to his front and his arm draped possessively over her waist, often cupping her mons.

She turned toward his side of the bed and smiled. Lying on his pillow was a beautiful lavender rose that had no thorns and a lovely fragrance. It had been positioned over a square thick paper with her name on it. Anne laid on her belly and turned it over; it had been folded into a pouch with a triangular flap. When she lifted it, she could see another piece of folded paper, which seemed to be enclosed in the pouch. She withdrew the piece of paper and read it.

Good morning, Anne,

I've gone downstairs to try and clear my day. I should be back in no time at all to spend the day with you. I'll bring breakfast with me so don't worry about it. There's chilled water in the fridge, and I left a couple of anti-inflammatories on the top. Don't take them until you've eaten something—there's fruit and muffins on the desk.

I left the Sterling Silver Rose as we just had an order arrive this morning. We don't get them very often, and I think they are beautiful, almost as beautiful as the woman with whom I spent my night.

Always,

Gabe

P.S. If you go to the door, make sure whatever you have on isn't see-through. I'm kind of possessive and territorial where my woman is concerned.

CHAPTER 17

H is woman? Anne smiled. She rather liked the sound of that. As she mused on his words, she heard a soft knock on the door. She grabbed one of the robes provided by the hotel, tied the sash around it so no one could see anything, and looked out the tiny round window in the door.

Opening the door, she said, "Good morning, my dear friend. I hope you didn't find yourself in too much trouble with Roark last night."

"Hmm, things must have gone well between you and Watson," Sage replied. "Roark was pissed I hadn't left him a note, which honestly I can't blame him for. Anything come up that you weren't sure about?"

"Not really. I'm glad we talked about how to prevent pregnancies. I would like to see someone about that pill you told me about. I was worried he'd find out we were at York Place, so I did admit we were in there, but I told him the jewels were missing."

Sage nodded. "That will work. Rachel said she hid them in a secure location. As soon as Holmes leaves in the morning, she'll get pictures of everything and bring them with her so we can give it to Nina. Rachel decided hiding them in the installed lockbox might not work as Holmes could easily find them. But she says to assure you they are safe. Nina texted me and will be here after lunch."

"Will it be okay if the address on my identification papers is different than where I am staying?"

"What's wrong with Rachel's old place?"

Anne grinned. "It isn't where Gabriel lives."

Sage laughed. "Geesh. That was fast. Anything else?"

"What's a fridge, and where is it in the room? Gabe said there was water, and something called anti-inflammatories."

"That rat bastard. He should have given you some of those last night. Apparently, he wanted the spanking and the make-up sex to have a lasting impression."

"Then he succeeded," said Anne.

Sage led her to the fridge and showed her how to open the water and the pill bottles.

Anne took a long drink of the water with the pills and then another long drink, enjoying both the cool-ness and the pure taste of the water. It was like enjoying a drink from a fresh spring hidden deep in the woods. "This is so good," she sighed.

"It's filtered so all of the impurities are gone, and making it cold helps a lot. Where is Gabe, by the way?"

"Down in his office. He's arranging to take the day off and spend it with me."

"That's fine to spend the day with Gabe, but we should move you tomorrow. Let me call Nina and make sure the change of address isn't bad. Once we have the ID, we can get the gems into a safety deposit box, which is like a private storehouse, only you can get into it much more easily than we did to the Ministry of Defence last night. Rachel, Saoirse or I can get the documents from Nina on your behalf."

Anne nodded, thinking the plan sounded perfect. "I did tell him our story about the abusive boyfriend, and he seemed to accept it," she added.

"Unfortunately, it's an all-too-common story…"

The phone on the desk rang, making Anne jump.

Sage's lips crinkled into a gentle frown. "Yeah, you really need to move tomorrow, and we need some time alone with you to show you some stuff so it doesn't scare you," she said. "That's a phone, another communication device like the mobile. Pick it up and hold the end with the cord close to your mouth and the other end by your ear. You can speak into it and hear and speak to the person on the other end of the call."

Anne carefully raised the phone to her ear as Sage had instructed. "Hello?" she asked.

"Anne, it's Gabe. Will you kill me if we can't move you in today? The hotel's got a big VIP coming in, and I need to be here."

"So, you don't want to sleep with me again?" she asked, stunned.

He'd lied! It shocked her, though she supposed it shouldn't have, knowing how every other man had treated her in her life. Why should this one be different? She felt her soul being crushed under the weight of her disappointment, which began to swiftly turn into red-hot anger.

"What are you talking about?" he growled.

"You fill my head with all kinds of foolish notions, just so you can spank me and then fuck me all night long," she said hotly, feeling used. "Really, Gabriel, if you were going to abandon me as soon as you left the room, why not just make it a clean break? Why bother with the rose and the note?" She could hear the near-hysterical tone in her voice, but she couldn't help it. He didn't want her after all...

"Because I love you," he explained. "You owe me ten tonight when I get up to the room."

"Ten?" she squeaked. "I can barely sit down... Wait, what did you say?"

He chuckled. "That I'm going to smack your ass ten times when I get up to your room tonight. I'll call when I'm leaving my office. I'll expect you to be sitting on the edge of the bed, naked."

"No, before that," she said, happiness filling her.

"I said I love you, but you're still getting spanked. As soon as I know when I'm going to be free, I'll order dinner to be sent up. Okay?"

"You really love me?"

"That's fifteen. Want to cast some more doubt my way?" he asked, calmly.

"No."

"That's twenty unless I hear the same coming back from you."

She smiled. "I love you too. I never thought I'd fall in love."

"Good to know. I'll see you later. Either call me or leave word with Felix or the desk if you decide to leave the hotel."

She agreed, then hung up the phone to end the call, her whole body warm at the thought of Gabe expressing his love for her.

Sage shook her head. "I never expected that. I mean it was pretty obvious that he was falling for you, but telling you he loves you this fast? Gabe's got it bad." She looked at Anne. "I suppose you do too, don't you?"

Anne shrugged, not ready yet to put it into words to anyone else. But she felt herself grinning widely. Sage smiled back, then raised her cell phone.

"I texted Nina, and she suggested it'd be best to

leave the documents at Rachel's, as Gabe might notice your ID has his address on it. And that would lead to unwanted questions."

"Agreed. Now what?" asked Anne, happier than she been since she'd watched Elizabeth ascend to the throne.

"Rachel's on her way up to the room. We'll work on contractions and technology."

"He won't really spank me again, will he?" Anne said, opening the door when she heard a knock.

"Every single chance he gets," said Rachel as she entered the room. "Holmes will use any excuse he can to see my ass turned vivid shades of pink and red. It gets him and me so turned on. They like seeing you squirm that night and especially the next day when it still hurts."

Sage laughed. "They want you to fall for them— telling you they love you, pledging their eternal devotion. But then they'll still spank you anyway, every chance they get. I've found that starting every day with 'good morning, Sir/Master. I love you' seems to put them in the right state of mind. By the way, Saoirse is on her way up. What's on the agenda for today?"

Anne was just turning to her when there was another knock, and in walked Saoirse.

"Felix told me that Gabe said you two are moving in together," she said, shaking her head at the speed of it all. "Rachel? Any chance I can buy your flat? I'm down here often enough, and I have always loved your place."

"That would be a great idea, Saoirse. After all, we love seeing you, but the Savoy is expensive for repeated stays." The two chatted a moment about it, and then Sage jumped in to get them back on course for the day's activities.

"We need to give Anne a crash course in modern technology," she announced. "And I think we need to get her a mobile as soon as Nina gets us the completed paperwork."

Anne spent the rest of the morning with her new friends, learning what her life would be like in this new century. Every once in a while, a shadow of fear would cross her mind, and she had no doubt it showed on her face. Each time it happened, either Saoirse, Sage or Rachel would reassure her, believing her emotions were simply nerves about launching into her new life.

She tried to encourage herself. Surely God, or whoever ruled these things, would not gift her with the life she had always wanted, only to have it taken away. But she couldn't shake her growing worry that inevitably, the Warder's dire warning would come to pass.

If he showed up again, Anne vowed not to return to the Tower. She would not allow the Warder of the Veil to accompany her to the Light. And if Azrael showed up, he had best be ready for a fight. She had gone to her death meekly to protect those members of her family she still loved—her father and uncle not among them. This time, she would not go so willingly.

As the other women showed her various devices and talked through modern wonders, Anne forced herself to let her worried thoughts of the Veil go, so she could pay attention to their instructions. If she did manage to stay in this present realm, she'd need to know all they were teaching her.

To help with modernizing her speech, familiarizing her knowledge of D/s relationships and to entertain her, Sage had given her an electronic reading device and downloaded a number of books onto it for her. Anne couldn't get over how easy this made it to learn new information.

They also introduced her to television—a most wondrous device that showed people acting in plays—but not within the confines of a theatre. People didn't need to utilize their imaginations; it was done for them. They found several movies about her daughter and then stumbled across a series that reportedly depicted King Henry VIII and his six wives. The problem was, the man looked nothing at all like Henry. He was shorter, much thinner and was far more handsome—and neither Catherine of Aragon nor Jane Seymour ever looked that good.

After the show about herself was over, Sage turned to her, eyes soft in concern. "Was it hard for you to watch your own execution?"

"Not really," Anne admitted. "It's strange, but that part of my life seems so distant. Interestingly enough, it was one of the few things that was portrayed accurately. And they did capture my father. He was devilishly handsome, an incredibly good diplomat and totally without a moral compass."

Nina Oletta came and went, delivering Anne's passport, birth certificate and national health card, promising to deliver the documents for the provenance of the gemstones and coins by the middle of next week.

Nina hadn't been gone a few minutes when Gabe cracked open the door. "Everyone decent?"

"Hardly," responded Sage, "but we all have our clothes on."

"Damn, and here I was hoping to get to see my woman naked and maybe do a little groping."

All four women laughed. It was obvious to anyone with eyes and half a brain that Gabriel Watson had fallen head over heels in love with Anne and vice versa.

"Was that Nina Oletta?" asked Gabriel.

"Yes," Anne told him. "I don't feel safe using my real last name or any identifying information. But if I want to get my health card, travel, get credit cards, or anything, I have to have them. I know that technically it's illegal, but I'm entitled to all of those things, and I won't be claiming them under my old name."

Gabe was quiet for a moment. "I don't disagree,

but it goes against my grain to be doing something illegal. We'll let it ride for a while and see if we can't come up with a better plan. I'm sorry about today."

"Me too," said Anne, rising up on her tiptoes to give his taciturn face a number of kisses. "But you'll be here tonight, right?"

Gabe folded her into his arms, kissing her soundly. "I probably won't get away until seven. Why don't I give you a call, and we'll try to have dinner downstairs again?"

"I'd like that."

She walked with Gabe to the door. He gave her a fond smile. "I just wanted to check in on you and make sure you were fine," he said.

She rocked up onto her toes and whispered, "No. You just wanted to make sure I'd welcome you back in my bed."

"And will you?" he asked earnestly.

"Always," she whispered.

After he left, Saoirse shook her head. "I swear, all three of you are just gaga over the men in your lives."

"Your point being?" asked Sage, saucily.

"That she's envious as hell that we all got our happily ever after," teased Rachel. "I really thought something might happen last night with Felix, though."

"Who's saying it didn't?" Saoirse retorted. "My problem is, I keep getting the distinct feeling that we're not out of the woods with Anne."

Anne took a deep breath. She would no longer lie to her friends. "The first night I was here, the Warder of the Veil paid me a visit." The ladies looked unhappy at the news, but not frightened.

"Did he try to harm you? We're pretty good at dealing with weird shit," said Sage.

Anne shook her head. "No. He was his usual kind self, urging me to return with him and let him lead me into the Light. But he also warned me that whatever powers govern these things are none too happy that I'm out. He warned me they would most likely send Azrael…"

"Who?" asked Rachel.

"Angel of Death," said Saoirse and Anne in unison.

"Aren't you afraid?" asked Sage.

"You need to tell Gabe," said Rachel.

"But if we tell him about Anne…" started Sage, a worried frown creasing her brow.

"We have to tell him about Holmes, Roark and Felix," said Rachel, nodding. "I get it. But he deserves to know. It bothers Holmes more and more that there's a secret that hangs between them. Saoirse gave him no choice about telling me. I was hurt and angry and then I got over it."

Anne shook her head. "I don't want him to know I'm some kind of freak."

"Gabriel would never think that of you. If he's going to be angry at anyone, it'll be Holmes—maybe

Roark and Felix, but Holmes will bear the brunt of it. The two of them are very close."

Anne shook her head, trying to negate what she knew to be the truth. "How exactly do I start that conversation? Oh, by the way, Watson, I used to be the Queen of England until Henry the VIII decided he wanted Jane Seymour and cut my head off."

Sage laughed, breaking the tension that had built in the room. "Okay, it does sound a bit odd when you put it that way."

"But if Saoirse is sensing something and this Warder fellow warned you, then I think we need to come clean with the lot of them. Don't you?" said Rachel, the last directed at Saoirse and Sage.

Saoirse agreed. "Aye. If there's trouble coming, there's not a better group of men to fight it than these four, especially with our help. But right now, we've tied one guy's hands behind his back... and I think we may have handicapped him more than we know."

"What do you mean?" asked Rachel.

"Remember the picture you showed me of Gabe's apartment? The one he took of the four of you in front of the fireplace?" Rachel nodded. "Something about it kept bugging me. I finally realized last night what it was. Felix and I worked on it all night. He's going to tell Roark and Holmes."

"What is it? Can I see?" asked Anne.

Rachel pulled out her phone and, after locating the picture, handed the mobile to Saoirse, who enlarged and focused it on the beautiful broadsword hanging over the large television.

"When I showed the picture to Felix, he said it was truly a work of art and has been in Gabriel's family for years," Saoirse said, handing the mobile to Anne, who gasped. "I'm right, aren't I?"

"If the pictures in the illuminated texts are accurate, then yes. That is *Courechouse* or the Holy Grand Blade—one of the legendary swords of the Knights of the Round Table," whispered Anne.

"The what?" asked Sage.

"It is said that *Courechouse* was forged by means of magick and alchemy. Its power is trumped only by one other sword, and it is said to have an almost infinite holy power capable of defeating the most powerful of demons," explained Anne.

"And another reason we have to tell Gabe," said Rachel. "That thing may well be the only thing that can defeat Azrael or at least force him back into the Void and make him leave Anne alone."

"Do you think he knows? In some ways, that might help," Anne said with a smile.

"How so?" asked Sage.

"Because it means he's keeping a secret as well. The only way he could have that sword is if he was a direct descendant of King Ban of Benwick, who was Sir Lancelot's father."

"Like King Arthur's Sir Lancelot?" asked Sage. "How do you know so much about it?"

"King Henry was very interested in the legend. And one of the gentlemen who was the closest to him was Henry Norris, the Groom of the Stool. He used to entertain Henry with tales of his ancestors. Henry became convinced that Norris had one of the legendary swords. I learned after my execution that most likely Cromwell included Norris in the list of those with whom I had committed adultery because Henry wanted the sword and Norris wouldn't give it up."

"But wasn't Norris a second son?" asked Rachel.

Anne nodded. "Legend says that the sword will choose its master, so it wasn't always the eldest son who got it. And more interestingly, if the Holy Grand Blade does not deem anyone worthy to wield it, like Excalibur, it disappears into the mists of time."

CHAPTER 18

*L*ater, Anne shooed her friends out and took the time to soak in the clawfoot tub, performed the grooming rituals that Rachel and Sage had recommended as Saoirse rolled her eyes and treated herself to an in-room mani/pedi. She afforded herself plenty of time and put on what she had planned to wear the night before. When she looked at herself in the mirror she thought, *Not bad for a woman of five hundred and twenty years.* Anne brought her hand to her mouth, resting her thumbnail against her bottom lip, and smiled.

For the first time since she had come through the Veil, she ventured out of her room on her own. She found it very empowering that she knew how to work the elevator to make it take her to the lobby. One of these would have come in handy during her first lifetime.

Gabe was waiting for her in the little foyer that connected the bank of elevators. "Hello, gorgeous," he said, greeting her as she stepped off. "You look amazing, and I love the nails."

"I have toes that match. The nice lady who did it for me called the color Cherry Mocha."

"I took the liberty of ordering for us," he said.

"Of course you did," she teased.

He led her into the restaurant. It was truly beautiful. Their table was secluded in a corner and by a window, which afforded them some extra privacy. Anne immediately liked the décor. Like most things in the Savoy, the room was elegant, but the restaurant also had a casual grace, combining large chandeliers with wood paneled walls, cream-colored tablecloths and fine table settings. The chairs were a comfortable mixture of leather and wood. Gabe held her chair and seated her with her back to the room, himself sitting where he had an exceptional view of the entire dining room.

"I ordered the Smoked Haddock Arnold Bennett Soufflé to start and the Classic Beef Wellington for us to share, with a Lemon-Raspberry Tart for dessert."

"It sounds wonderful. I've never had any of those, but I would love cheeseburgers with fries if I were eating them with you."

Gabe laughed. "Now you're making me nervous. You meet me down here looking like every fantasy I've ever had, and you tell me as long as you're with me, you'll trade five-star food for a backyard barbecue."

"I would indeed," she said, smiling before leaning across to kiss him. "I've missed you today."

"And I you," he said, taking her hand, bringing it to his lips and kissing it. "I never thought I'd feel this way about anyone."

"Me either. I didn't believe that real people could experience a love like this. Do you think we could either skip dessert or take it with us?"

"Sure, babe. I can get them to package it up for us."

"Take me home, Gabriel. I want to see your place. I want to sleep in your bed… Well, technically, I want to fuck in your bed, eat our dessert, fuck some more and then sleep."

He laughed, the sound laced with humor and lust. "Whether we're here at the hotel or home in our flat, you still owe me fifteen."

"Gabe…"

Gabe shook his head. "You deserve the ten, but I'll forgive the other five."

"Rachel said Holmes uses any excuse to spank her," she said, pouting.

"Do you think I did anything to deserve you going off on me like that when I called you earlier?"

Anne realized he had a point. "No I don't. I do apologize."

"Forgiven, or it will be later tonight. That's the

thing about discipline; it allows me to express my anger or disappointment at your behavior and makes you consider better options for the next time."

"And the great sex afterwards?"

"Our way of atoning to each other—you for acting out and me for having to discipline you because of it."

Gabe had the waitstaff package up their dessert, paid the bill and escorted her to his car. This was Anne's first time riding up front, and she thoroughly enjoyed it. She could see better out the window, and it was delightful to see everything lit up by the marvelous electricity that this century had at its disposal. As they passed by the Millennium Wheel, or the Eye as most Londoners called it, Anne asked, "Can we go on that sometime?"

"You've never been?" She shook her head. "Are you afraid of heights?"

"When I am with you, I fear nothing. And no matter the cost, I wouldn't trade being with you for anything."

Gabe gave her a quizzical look as she turned her head to look out the window. They were in Soho in no time at all, and he parked his black Range Rover in its assigned spot. They took the restored freight elevator to his top floor flat. He opened the door and was a bit taken aback when their friends were all gathered round.

He looked down at Anne. "You're back up to fifteen, princess."

"I was never a princess," she said, drawing herself up the same way she had the first time he'd seen her.

Gone was the relaxed, elegant and sensual woman he'd fallen for. In her place was a regal beauty whose icy stare could drop a man to his knees. He heard someone move in behind him, between him and the door. It was Felix. There was no way Felix should ever have been able to block his path to an exit.

Gabe sighed. He really had gone soft on Anne to be missing such things.

"What's going on?" he said, catching Anne by the arm before she could put any distance between them.

Anne turned to Sage and Rachel, "The rest of them know the truth?"

Rachel nodded. "Yes, we told them."

"What truth?" Gabriel growled. "What the hell is going on, Anne. What haven't you told me?"

"This isn't her fault," said Holmes.

"What isn't?" asked Gabe.

"Gentlemen," said Roark. "Why don't we all just take a seat and discuss this like civilized individuals and friends?"

"It's going to be all right, Watson," said Rachel.

"What's going to be all right?" Gabe asked. Accommodating his friend's request, he sat down in one of his leather wingbacks and pulled Anne onto his lap. She made a half-hearted struggle to get free. "Want to try for twenty?" he asked, never taking his eyes off Felix, Holmes and Roark. Anne relaxed and allowed him to hold her close to his chest.

"Holmes, sweetheart? I've just been through this," Rachel said. "More than anyone, I'm going to know how he feels."

"Somebody needs to tell me what the fuck is going on because I'm beginning to get a little freaked."

Rachel, who was sitting next to Holmes, leaned forward. "Do you remember when we fought the Ripper?" Gabe nodded. "Remember how unsettling it was to realize there really are supernatural forces at work all around us?"

"Did that thing get loose again? I thought you said the banshees dragged it to Hell." Gabe turned to Anne. "I'll explain everything. I probably should have before."

"Don't," she whispered, placing her three middle fingers over his lips. "You have nothing to apologize for."

"She's right," said Holmes, who stared at him imploringly.

Gabe leaned closer to his best friend. "Tell me."

"Remember when Sage and Roark got involved?"

"Yeah, her old publisher was trying to kill her," said Gabe. "What has that got to do with anything paranormal?"

"Everything," said Sage.

"It was only after Sage arrived in London that Felix, Roark and I existed outside the pages of Sage's books," said Holmes.

"What the fuck do you mean by that?" asked Gabe in disbelief.

"Before the threat to Sage's life drew Felix and me through the Veil, we had no corporeal form. And it took a direct threat on her life to give Roark the energy to pierce the Veil himself and save her."

Watson shook his head. What nonsense were they trying to tell him? His friends weren't spirits or hobgoblins. He'd known them for years. "Holmes, you're talking nonsense. Anne, is this some kind of joke or pretense to get you out of the discipline you're owed?"

"I wish it was, sweetheart. I would endure the worst spanking you could give me many times over if I could spare you this upset."

That rattled him. The earnestness of her voice, the tears welling in her eyes. "It's true?" he whispered, afraid of her response. "Tell me I'm not going to lose you over this."

In that moment, he realized that she was what truly mattered. If she couldn't handle whatever it was, they'd leave together, maybe move back to Chicago and never look back.

Anne took his face in her hands. "I would never,

ever willingly leave you. I have waited an eternity to find you, and I won't give you up without a fight."

He turned back to look at Holmes. "It's true? The three of you are some kind of supernatural beings?"

Holmes nodded. "We should have told you long ago, but at first we didn't understand it and were a bit freaked to find ourselves here. There were so many times I wanted to tell you, but I didn't know how. Then I realized I had to tell Rachel and felt even worse excluding you. Gabe, you are my closest friend. You have to forgive me." Holmes' tone of voice implored him to accept the impossible and to embrace the man who felt like his oldest and best friend.

"I guess it would seem kind of wussy if Rachel could handle it and I couldn't," he said, trying to ease the tension in the room.

"That's the stuff, Watson," said Felix.

"I have always known there was something weird about you," he said, grinning at Felix.

"I feel the same way about you."

"Why did they tell you?" he asked Anne.

"Because I'm like them."

"You came out of a book?"

"Hundreds of them," said Rachel with a warm smile.

Anne waved her off. "Rachel is incorrect. I did not enter this world by piercing the Veil between fiction and reality."

Gabe laughed, hoping to God she wasn't about to tell him he'd fallen for some kind of spirit with a predetermined shelf life.

"I was able to pierce the Veil between Life and the Void."

"The what?" he asked, almost afraid to hear the explanation.

"When you die, especially a violent death, your spirit is sometimes allowed to transition through the Void to allow you to process what happened. The Void exists between Life and either the Light or the Darkness. In the Light, you abide in eternal peace and joy. In the Darkness, there is only torment."

"So, how long were you in this Void?"

"Almost five hundred years."

"That's bullshit, Anne. You don't look a day over four hundred."

She smiled. "Not funny. I was beheaded on Tower Hill on May 19, 1536."

"That was during the reign of Henry VIII, wasn't it?" he said, turning to Rachel, who nodded.

"What, you were Anne of Cleaves?"

"No, sweetheart. Anne of Cleaves was the smart one. She managed to survive marriage to Henry without having to endure being bedded or raped by him. She ended up a wealthy woman."

"The only other Anne was…"

Anne nodded and held up her hand. "See? I only have five fingers, not six."

"You're… you're…"

"I am Anne Boleyn, Queen of England and Henry VIII's second wife."

The silence sat between them like billowing, dense fog that took its time dissipating.

"This isn't a joke, is it?" he whispered.

"No. I'm afraid it isn't. I didn't know how to tell you…" she started.

Gabe removed her from his lap and walked across the room to the window, before turning back to them.

"Do you know what you've done to me?" he asked, rubbing his forehead as if he had a headache. "One minute, I'm this guy who's finally found a life of his own and escaped a past that was less than pleasant. Against all odds, I found my perfect soul mate, only there's one tiny little problem. None of it is real. My best friends are all specters of some sort, and the woman I'm in love with is a ghost. Jesus, is any of this even real? Have I gone completely insane?"

"I'm not a ghost, Gabriel. I'm real," Anne insisted, she said reaching out for him and then pulling her hand back. "You've had your hands all over me. Hell, you've had your cock and tongue all over and in me. Could a ghost's cunt have squeezed your cock the way mine did repeatedly last night? Could a ghost call your name as you ruthlessly fucked her to orgasm after orgasm? Could a ghost have been such an avid student of learning to worship your amazing cock?"

Gabe waved them all away, dismissing them. "I think you should all leave. I need some time to think. Leave. *Now*."

The others paused, unsure what to do. Anne looked heartbroken, but Gabe steeled himself to ignore her pleading gaze. Roark rose and began to shoo everyone out the door.

"Come on," he said to them as he ushered them out. "We can head back to the hotel and have a drink. Gabriel will know where to find us." Everyone reluctantly left, Felix looking sorry, Holmes miserable, Anne... No, he refused to look in her direction, or he might break.

Once he was the last one inside the flat, alone with Gabe, Roark turned and said, "Be angry with us if you want, Watson. We've been your friends for a long time and chose not to tell you. But Anne has only been in this world since All Hallows Eve. She didn't beg for her life as she walked to the scaffold; I doubt she will beg for your love. If you let her leave here, I'm not sure she won't just go back to the Tower and surrender herself to her fate."

Gabe studied him, confused and seeking an answer. "What do you mean by that?"

"The first night she was at the Savoy, the Warder of the Veil, a kind of guardian who helps those like Anne who are trapped in the Void find their way to the Light, visited her and pleaded for her to return with him and pass on. He warned her that if she didn't come of her own volition that night, he might not be able to save her from Azrael, the Angel of Death, who would come to drag her into eternal Darkness."

"Get out, Roark." This was bullshit—regardless of whether any of it were true or not. Either his friends and the woman he'd given his heart to had lied to him or this was some kind of bizarre game that he wasn't equipped to play.

Roark refused to move. "Anne recognized your sword," he said, pointing to where it hung over the fireplace. "She says it will only serve a warrior of the Light. So tell me, my friend—and never doubt that's who and what you are to me—will you let the Angel of Death have the woman you love and drag her into Hell?"

"The sword?" Gabe glanced at it, then turned back to Roark, puzzled.

"Yes. Anne says it is the Holy Grand Blade, more powerful than even Excalibur. If it is now in your hands, the sword means for you to wield it to fight for the Light. I believe it called Anne forward to fight by your side. If anyone knows about injustice and how power can corrupt absolutely, it would be the beheaded wife of the monster known as Henry VIII."

CHAPTER 19

*G*abe stood for the longest time, staring at the sword above his fireplace. He'd come across it in an old antique store in Cornwall. He'd never been all that keen on swords, but something about the blade had called to him. So, he purchased it, hung it above his 52" television and never gave it a second thought.

Until now.

He reached up and even before he touched the hilt, he could feel the blade begin to vibrate. Small electrical charges flashed out, striking his hand, daring him to grasp the handle of the sword and lift it from the cradle in which it had hung still and silent for so many years.

〜

"Give him time, Anne," counseled Rachel as she walked with her arm around the broken queen and helped her into one of the two SUVs they had driven to Gabriel's flat.

Worried but unable to do anything else right now, Anne simply nodded and rode back to the hotel with the others, lost in her thoughts. She liked what she had seen of his home. It was small, but with room enough for two. And like the Savoy Grill, his dwelling showed a casual elegance and innate comfort that had called to her. She'd had time to study the sword above his television, and she was certain it was the Holy Grand Blade. Gabriel was its master, but he had no idea the kind of power for good he could wield with it.

They arrived back at the Savoy and made their way quietly up to their respective floors. Saoirse and Sage accompanied Anne, who had never felt more alone, even though she knew that wasn't the truth. She had found a lot of what she had never known in her previous life in her short time in this world— friends who cared deeply and truly for her and the grand love she had always dreamed of.

Even when she had faced death, she hadn't felt devoid of all life and light. She had faced her death with the same strong will and passion she had given to her life. But Gabriel's rejection of her felt as if he had reached inside her body cavity, grasped her entrails, jerked them out and set them ablaze.

"I thought I was being given a second chance," she confessed as they headed toward the room where, just a few hours earlier, she'd been so happy. "I thought I would get to live the life I chose, free from the encumbrances of men. Then I met Gabriel and found myself willing to submit, not to men in general, but to this one man, and he pushed me away. Maybe that's why I got to break free of the Void, to learn that there was nothing for me here."

"Don't say that Anne," said Saoirse. "Give him time. For the rest of us, we've had that time to get used to the idea. For poor Gabe, he has just found out his closest friends have not been truthful with him and that the woman he loves used to be Queen of England."

"A queen who only wanted the crown because I refused to become just another discarded mistress. That's the funny part you know. I never wanted the crown. My father did. My uncle did. But I would have been happy to be married to a not so powerful man, living an ordinary life. Instead, I was thrust into a world not of my liking nor of my making. The real irony is, Henry cast me away more easily than he did any of the others. I thought the crown would save me. But in the end, it proved to be my downfall."

At the door, she stopped. "I'd like a little time alone. You two and Rachel have given me something I never thought to have—true friends who wanted nothing from me other than my friendship. And that, you will always have." Squeezing their hands in thanks, she left them in the hall.

Anne walked into her room and looked around, knowing what she had to do. When she had faced the executioner's blade, she had stroked Henry's ego one last time and put the needs of her daughter, her family, her people and her country ahead of her own need for revenge. She knew that history had portrayed her as a power-hungry seductress who cared for no one but herself. But nothing could be further from the truth.

The Warder had warned her that if Azrael had to come and drag her back, he would damn her soul to eternal darkness. He had also made it clear that those around her could be in danger. And she would not allow her sins to rob those she had come to care for of their lives, their loves or their happiness. As much as she wanted this life, she did not want it without Gabriel. So it was not meant to be. And if she could not have a life here with him, it would be best to give herself up to the Warder and finally allow him to guide her to the Light.

Anne sat on the edge of the bed. She changed out of the little black dress she had purchased to entice Gabriel. Instead, the dress had become the outfit she wore when she lost him. So, now, it had no place it her life. Leaving it on the floor, she changed into the comfortable sweater, soft, faded jeans and hunting boots she had so enjoyed wearing yesterday, and waited for the quiet of deep night to fall.

When Big Ben struck two, she made her way back to the Tower of London. The streets were dark, mostly empty save for the occasional homeless person or unsavory character hiding in the shadows. But she was not afraid of them. After all, she'd died once, and she was about to return to the Void and die again. That wasn't technically true. If Watson didn't love her, she was already dead. The pain of that possibility clutched at her heart as nothing else ever had. There was no longer anything that could touch her.

She began to make her way down to the Traitor's Gate. The last time she had entered the fortress, it had been through that portal. Now, how the hell was she supposed to get inside? The thought had no sooner formed than she heard the Traitor's Gate creak as it swung open. It seemed her destiny awaited her.

Gabriel tossed and turned as sleep eluded him. The night before, he had slept in Anne's arms and peace had enveloped him. He had just sat up in bed and swung his legs over the side, giving up on resting anytime soon, when there was a loud knocking on his door.

"Gabriel! Gabriel!" screamed Rachel.

He glanced at the clock. It was two-thirty in the

morning. What the hell was his best friend's fiancée doing pounding on his door and disturbing the neighbors? As he stumbled toward the door dressed only in his boxers, he realized that's who Rachel was —not just a noted expert in the Tudor dynasty, not only a successful businesswoman and friend to Sage and Saoirse, but his best friend's—*best* friend's— fiancée.

Gabe threw open the door, and Rachel flung herself in his arms. "Get dressed and grab that damn sword," she demanded.

Gabe wrapped his arms around her and twirled her around. "Slow down a sec—"

"For God's sake, you idiot, put me down and get some pants on. Holmes is turning the car around, not easy on these skinny little cobblestone streets."

"What is it?" he said.

"Just hurry!"

Setting her down, he went back into his bedroom and pulled on a pair of jeans, socks and boots. Grabbing a sweater, he walked back to the living area where Rachel stood trying to wrestle the sword out of its hanger. He pulled the sweater on and reached over her, easily taking the sword in hand.

"Anne was right," she said. "The blade knows its master. Anne seems to have forgotten hers."

Gabe shook his head, not following her panicked words. "Holmes is downstairs? Where is Anne?"

"Yes, Holmes is waiting for us! And I fear the love

of your life is headed for the Tower to give herself up to the Light."

"Why would she do that?"

Rachel rolled her eyes. "Because, you dolt, without you, she had nothing in this life that she wanted."

Gabe rocked back on his heels at her vehemence. "And the sword?"

"I hope you know how to use that thing, because if Saoirse is right, and she always is about stuff like this, you're going to have to fight the Angel of Death to get your girl back."

"What the fuck!" he snarled. He grabbed Rachel by the arm and ran with her down to the street where Holmes was waiting with the car doors open. He tossed Rachel into the seat behind him. Then he grabbed Holmes in an enormous bear hug.

"Forgive me."

"No time for that. We need to go save your girl. God save us from women who want to be noble." Holmes said, looking at Rachel in the rearview mirror.

"Hey, it worked out for us."

"Where are the others?" asked Gabe, knowing full well Roark, Sage, Saoirse and Felix had not abandoned him.

"At the Tower. Trying to find a way in. And Saoirse is gathering a mist to keep whatever happens away from prying eyes and ears."

Holmes used his lights, but no sirens, to all but fly through the streets of London. They spotted Felix down by the Thames. Holmes parked the SUV and the three of them followed Felix to Traitor's Gate.

"With this fog, I blind from hearing and sight,
All that doth occur this night."

Over and over, Saoirse repeated the spell, holding her arms up toward the moon, entreating its power to help her. The ever-present fog in the city heard and obeyed, rising up from the river below to shield the fortress that was the Tower of London. Within moments, they were surrounded.

"One little question… How are we supposed to see?" asked Felix.

"You know so little about magick. Those with me on this quest will be able to penetrate the fog—and glad to see Watson that you're back with us. You are, aren't you?" asked Saoirse.

"If the Angel of Death thinks he's going to take my woman, he'd best think again. I will defend her with every last breath in my body," declared Gabe. "Holmes, you once told me if it went wrong, I should get Rachel and run. I'm charging you with the same promise. If I can't defeat him, I will hold him off. Grab Rachel and Anne and get them to safety."

"Fuck that shit," said Holmes, straightening his

shoulders. "I'm staying to fight with my best friend. We'll beat this SOB and dance on his grave."

The four of them darted through the gate and into the open ground that was Tower Green. In the middle of Tower Green, Anne stood facing two figures that were more opaque than solid. One wore the uniform of an old-time Yeoman Warder and held an eight-foot long halberd—the Warder of the Veil. The other figure, presumably the Angel of Death, bore a scythe, his dark robe and hood obscuring his visage.

"Your friends have come to die with you," Azrael intoned, his voice deep and unshakable. Anne looked behind her, her gaze seeking Gabe's face. Then she straightened her backbone and turned toward the Angel of Death, imperious as a queen.

"No," argued Anne. "The Warder of the Veil said if I returned of my own volition, my friends would be spared, and I could go into the Light. I am here and ready to surrender myself to the Light."

"I fear you are too late," said the Warder, his eyes kind but saddened.

"You and your friends are mine," cackled Azrael.

"New deal," snapped Gabe. "How about you and I tangle? Your scythe against me and *Courechouse*. You win, you take us both to the Darkness. We win, you take your smelly robes—what is that? Fire and brimstone?—and go fuck yourself in the Darkness, while me and mine go home, never again to be bothered by either of you." He turned to look at the Warder. "If you won't give her up, you'll have to take us both. From now on we're a package deal."

Tears welling in her eyes, Anne said, "What makes you think I'll have you?"

Gabe grinned at her. "That's twenty," he warned. "And I don't recall asking your opinion. Now go stand behind Roark and Holmes."

Anne lifted her chin and shook her head. "No. You told them we were a package deal. I stand with you."

With an unholy screech, Azrael swung the scythe at Anne. Gabe shoved her out of the way, using *Courechouse* to deflect the blade. He was impressed with himself. It had been a long time since he'd handled a sword and never one that had this kind of magickal power. There were others he knew, but he hadn't recognized *Courechouse* for what it was that afternoon in Cornwall. Out of the corner of his eye, he saw the Warder of the Veil directing the halberd at Anne, Gabe whirled with the sword, bringing it under the halberd, swinging upwards and disarming the Warder of the Veil.

"Damn it, Anne, get behind Roark and Holmes."

"No."

"That's twenty-five and get behind me then."

Anne made a grab for the halberd and managed to snag it just before the Warder of the Veil got it back under his control. As the Angel of Death swung the scythe toward him, there was a swoosh, but Gabe ducked under it and thrust the sword at Azrael, forcing him backwards. *Courechouse* had a long handle that allowed for a two-fisted grip, giving the wielder additional power. The blade itself seemed to glow in the dark night, and he could feel its strength and might.

He saw Holmes grab the halberd from Anne and push her toward Roark, who lifted her off the ground, kicking and screaming as he retreated to the gate where he and Felix could keep the women safe.

"I say, Watson," intoned Holmes as he stepped up beside his friend. "I do believe *the game is afoot*."

"You're an idiot," said Gabe with a grin.

Holmes smiled determinedly and nodded. Gabe nodded back. Together, they began an aggressive assault on both the Warder of the Veil and the Angel of Death.

"If you can force them back through the doorway of the Queen's House, they won't be able to pierce the Veil and escape the Void to come after Anne," called Saoirse.

"Which one is the Queen's House?" called Holmes, who continued to hold off the Warder of the Veil while Gabe was involved in a deadly and pitched battle with the Angel of Death.

"Directly behind you," screamed Anne. "Let go of me!"

What had once felt awkward—the sword in his

hands—now began to feel familiar. Gabe realized that swinging *Courechouse* was much like wielding a flogger, although considerably heavier. It made him more confident in his movements and it showed in his successful countering of the spectral creature's every move. He knew the moment the battle turned, as Azrael began keeping the scythe closer to his body and his movements were defensive, not offensive. Gabe continued his attack, forcing the Angel of Death to retreat. It screeched at him—unintelligible sounds that hurt his ears—but Gabe continued to relentlessly swing *Courechouse*.

In his peripheral vision, he saw Holmes had the Warder of the Veil in retreat as well. Both specters were losing to the two mortals, who were fighting for the women they loved. Over and over, Gabe swung *Courechouse* until he had Azrael's back to the darkened opening of the Queen's House. With a mighty lunge, he pierced the Angel of Death's robes, forcing him inside.

Then, he stepped aside as Holmes marched the Warder of the Veil through the opening.

"My halberd, Sir?" the Warder asked politely from the other side of the Veil.

"Don't think so. Spoils of war. Who knows when we might need it again?"

"You will not need to fight us again," said the Warder.

"Why do you say that?" asked Watson.

The Warder smiled. "Spoils of war. Your lady has proven her worth and has bested both Azrael and I. She has defeated those who would have damned her to the Void or to the Darkness. By having those that would risk their lives for her, she has earned her place back amongst the living."

"So, she's free of you?" asked Watson suspiciously. "They won't send you or anyone else to try and snatch her back?"

"She is free. She has proven herself—by her courage and strength of heart—to be deserving of a second life. There are only a few others who have been able to do the same. Love your lady well. She deserves a life where she is cherished. Tell her I will miss her grace and beauty."

Gabe nodded. "I will."

The two friends watched as the Warder slowly turned his back and vanished into the Void; then they wrapped their arm around the other's shoulder and headed back to their friends.

"Come on," said Saoirse. "The spell isn't going to hold forever, and we need to be out of here when the fog lifts."

CHAPTER 20

The four couples raced to the SUVs. Holmes, Gabe, Rachel and Anne got in one; Roark, Felix, Sage and Saoirse in the other.

"Roark will get them back to the Savoy," said Holmes. "I thought I'd take you back to Soho."

"I probably should have squeezed in with Roark. It will be out of your way, won't it, to take me back to the Savoy?"

Anne saw Rachel shake her head as Roark said to Gabe, "She thinks she's going back to the Savoy."

"She's wrong," said Gabe amiably.

"That's it?" asked Anne. "They hate each other, then fight a common enemy and poof, they're friends again?"

"Pretty much," said Gabe. "I told you once, babe, we're guys. We're like that."

"That's bullshit." Anne turned to look at Rachel. "That's the right word, isn't it?"

"Right word, but I don't think Gabe is the one you want to say it in front of," said Rachel, patting her hand.

"Why not? I'm nothing to him. He cast me out. We haven't even known each other a week, and I don't tell him every little thing about me, and he pitches a fit and throws me out."

"Not true, sweetheart. I threw everyone else out. And I apologize. I should have kept you on my lap, and I should never have thrown my friends out. Thank God they're the forgiving type. If it weren't for them, I might have lost you."

"Nah," said Holmes. "You might have spent forever with her in eternal darkness, but I'm not sure they could have held you that long."

"They only wanted me," said Anne.

Gabe turned and pierced her with his icy blue stare. "Do you really think I would have let them have you? Do you honestly believe I wouldn't have stormed the gates of Hell to get you back? Careful how you answer. You owe me twenty-five. Answer correctly and I'll wipe the slate clean. Answer incorrectly and you owe me fifty. Double or nothing, Anne. What's it to be?"

Anne's smile could have lit up not only the SUV, but all of London as well. "I love you, Gabriel Watson. I couldn't face the prospect of living in this world without you. I thought since I just wanted to die, I'd at least keep you and my friends safe."

Gabe unfastened his seatbelt and turned around, taking her face in his hands. "I love you, Anne Watson. If Nina Oletta is doing identity papers, we may as well get them done right the first time."

"Hmm, Anne Watson who lives in Soho. Has a nice ring. But you know, the last man who married me gave me a crown."

Gabe laughed. "He also cut off your head."

"True enough. So, Anne Watson it is."

∼

Twelve Weeks Later
Gabe and Anne's Soho Loft
London, England

Anne whirled around to look at him. Had he really just said what she thought he had?

"What do you mean you want to take me to a dungeon? Good God Gabe, even Henry didn't throw me in a dungeon!"

"What?" Gabe said, confused and then enlightenment hit him, and he started laughing.

This was really the only downfall of having fallen in love with a woman who was considerably older than he was…485 years older to be precise.

"I don't find the idea of you tossing me in a

dungeon or even visiting one to be humorous," she said, drawing herself up.

He wondered if she knew how adorable he found her when she drew herself up and addressed him in a regal tone. Gabe had learned that she only did so when she was feeling unsure of herself or what he was talking about. He tried to remember that they were often two people separated by a common language— American and English. And it didn't help that her English was from the time of the Tudors.

"I'm not laughing at you, and I would never take you anywhere that made you uncomfortable. Well, that's not technically true. D/s is all about pushing boundaries and finding out how much pleasure I can give you. And you, my beautiful queen, are capable of so much more than anyone ever guessed. Henry was indeed a fool if he could not see that. But I am not Henry."

"But you said…"

He cut her off with a kiss, lowering his mouth to hers and thrusting his tongue between her lips. Gabe had found this was an effective way to head off a tirade. One of the few things her contemporaries had been right about was Anne's passionate nature. She wrapped her arms around his neck and melted into him.

When he released her mouth, he looked down at her. "I'm sorry, sweetheart. I sometimes forget that there are certain words that are triggers for you. I should have figured that out. The dungeon I'm talking about is Baker Street."

"The club? Why would you call it that?"

"Because most people refer to a BDSM club, especially the sceneing areas as a dungeon. There may be people tied up or having a whip or flogger used on them, but it is completely and totally consensual. I thought you might enjoy it."

He loved the wicked little smile turning up the corners of her mouth and how her eyes danced with merriment. "Hmmm... as I understand it, I need a certain kind of apparel to appear on the dungeon floor."

"Yes you do. And no doubt Rachel and Sage have told you all about The Dark Garden."

"They may have mentioned it. They also mentioned that the owner is a bobolyne."

Gabe laughed. "A what?"

"A fool. What merchant wouldn't want women coming in to buy things that incite their husbands into fits of lust."

"Probably thinking said Dom would want to be consulted before a sub dropped that kind of money on an outfit."

"I wouldn't ask you to pay for it. I have my own money and what we already have we can't spend in our lifetime, and we haven't even looked at what the gemstones would bring."

Anne was right. They had been able to trade most

of the coins she'd managed to smuggle out of the Void for a small fortune in modern currency. Gabe had made her a signatory on his accounts, but he also wanted her to have a separate account so she could learn to manage money and wouldn't feel as if she had to ask permission for everything. Interestingly enough, of the four women who were close friends— Anne, Rachel, Saoirse and Sage—Anne was the best with money.

"True enough, but its Louis' store and he is entitled to run it as he sees fit."

"I have a good mind to tell him what I think of it. He shouldn't be allowed to tell a woman she can't buy what she wants."

"He isn't. He's telling subs they can't buy fet wear in his shop. There are other shops, which your friends all know about. The four of you have just got it into your heads that he's going to do what you want him to do the way you want him to do it. And in case it's missed your notice, a sub telling a Dom how he's going to do something doesn't generally go over well. Maybe taking you to Baker Street is a bad idea."

"No, Gabriel. I want to go. I know you like it and Sage and Rachel say it's wonderful. I want to go."

"Do you think you can behave if we go to the Dark Garden?"

"Yes, Gabriel," she said contritely.

He shook his head. "Why oh why do I think this is going to be a royal clusterfuck?"

It didn't take them long to get to the Dark Garden and the proprietor greeted them warmly. What some of the subs didn't understand was that Louis truly loved women and loved making them look and feel sexy and beautiful. He just didn't want to see them get into trouble with their Doms either for spending too much money or buying something the Dom would deem inappropriate.

"Gabriel," Louis greeted them, trying to take Anne's hands into his to kiss her cheeks.

"Don't," Anne said coolly.

"Anne doesn't like men she doesn't know touching her," explained Gabe, before turning to her. "Be nice. I told you, Louis was going to have to take your measurements to fit you properly."

"I would prefer a woman."

She was drawing herself up.

"No one measures the subs, except for me. I have women who sew for me, but I am the master corsetiere."

Gabe hated admitting it, but Louis was kind of a pain. Problem was, Gabe was pretty sure the trans-planted Frenchman had never dealt with a former Queen of England.

"Then, Gabriel, I would prefer to go elsewhere," she said regally and turned to go. "I'll be sure to tell them at Baker Street tonight how I was treated today. 'Tis a shame as I was thinking we might find one that could be tailored to fit me and then order several others, but I only allow my Dom's hands on me, not some overreaching Frenchman."

"Anne," Gabriel said warningly. "Behave yourself."

"Do you really want that grubbing little Frenchman to grope me? I had enough of that at... a long time ago."

Anne stood her ground. Gabe knew she would not yield.

"Louis, might you have a female fitter that you could supervise taking Anne's measurements?"

"You would let her speak to me that way?"

"I would. She asked for a female fitter as she doesn't like any man's hands on her except mine. I have to tell you, I'm not overly fond of the idea either. If you don't have someone, I understand, but I will let Anne have her way on this."

They were at a stalemate. Gabe understood where Louis was coming from, but he also wanted Anne to feel she had control. From what she had shared, and he knew he didn't yet have the whole story, she'd been a pawn to be used by men her entire life. She yielded to him, but not to others. In fact, he rather enjoyed watching her go a few rounds with Roark. She was highly intelligent and had a quick and sharp wit.

"I suppose. I have been teaching my niece, but I will need to be there to ensure it is done correctly."

"Thank you, Louis," Anne said graciously. "I appreciate you accommodating me."

"But of course," Louis said, completely beguiled by her. "Would you prefer to have Gabriel with us? Some women are uncomfortable with their Dom seeing them, but I suspect you bask in his attention."

Anne smiled and Gabe wasn't sure, but he thought Louis might have blushed. He led them into one of the fitting rooms and Gabe sat in one of the comfortable chairs. Louis ducked out of the door, closing it behind him.

"I take it I'm to sit in your lap?" she asked archly.

"Or on the floor at my feet or you can always lay across my lap and get your bottom spanked," he returned.

She sighed. "I suppose I'll sit in your lap."

It never ceased to amaze him how incredibly graceful she was. She lowered herself with all the elegance and poise of a prima ballerina deigning to sit in his lap. His cock jumped in his trousers the minute she alighted, and she grinned.

"Don't be thinking naughty thoughts."

She batted her lashes at him, "But, Sir, I'm sure I don't know what you're talking about."

Louis returned carrying several bolts of material, followed by a young woman carrying several corsets as well as a basket full of trimmings.

"I think with Anne's coloring, the obvious thing would be red. But I think purple. After all, it is the color of royalty and certainly she is your queen," said Louis.

"I keep telling him that," Anne said, and then practically salivated as his niece showed her a pre-made corset.

"I saw that material and had to make it up. I believe it would be close and very easily tailored to your lady by adding a bit of black lace at the hem and perhaps a black lace placard down the front as well as straps."

"Louis, it's gorgeous. Gabe?"

"I agree. But then I think you look beautiful in anything… or nothing at all."

Anne looked at Louis, conspiratorially, "Doms."

"*Oui, mais tu l'aimes.*"

"I fear, my dear Louis, you are right."

"*Je t'aime,*" responded Gabriel.

"He speaks the language fluently," said Anne. "I found that out the hard way when I cursed at him in French."

Louis laughed, now completely enchanted by her. "You should know better than to swear at your Dom."

"Yes, one of those silly rules you Doms have—no cursing, no panties and the whole being bare below. Although that last one is rather fun when he does it."

Louis and his niece both laughed.

The rest of the fitting went easily, and Louis sent the purple corset back to one of his seamstresses to do the alterations. Once he had Gabe's permission, he and Anne chose several different fabrics for her corsets and matching thongs. Louis' niece took Anne's measurements and by the time they left, Louis was treating Anne like the queen she was.

As they left the store, Gabe said, "Catherine of Aragon had nothing on you. Henry was never worthy of you."

"I love you. I thought I loved Henry, but I was wrong. I love you in a way I never even imagined was possible."

"Right back at you. I need to run by the office for a minute, want to come along?"

"Yes, please," she purred.

Gabe groaned. He had a sneaky suspicion he was about to be manipulated in a way he liked very much. They entered the Savoy and headed into his office. Anne followed him in, closed the door and locked it. Before he could say anything, she molded herself to his body, wrapping her arms around his neck and standing on her tiptoes offering her mouth to him.

There were times he absolutely couldn't resist her and today was one of them, although she had learned she could go only so far. He lowered his head, his mouth capturing hers as his tongue slipped inside, dancing with hers as she moaned. He brought one hand up between them to caress her breasts, thumbing the turgid nipple he found there. With his other hand, he rucked up her dress exposing her bare pussy to his touch.

Anne shivered in his embrace as she moaned under the onslaught of his kiss. He walked them back to his desk, sweeping aside the paperwork on it as he laid her back, parting her legs as he did so in order to be standing between them. He pulled down the wide neckline and unfastened her bra so that he could dip his head and draw her nipple into his mouth.

"Gabe, yes," she purred. "I thought I was going to die."

Gabe kissed his way back up her throat, stopping to push her hair aside and nuzzle the scar that remained from where the blade had first engaged her neck. He stiffened.

"It's all right, sweetheart, I'm here. I'm alive. I'm with you."

"It's a good thing Henry is dead. If he wasn't, I'd kill the bastard."

He kissed his way back down, capturing her pebbled peak in his mouth, gently nipping it before licking around the areola and then popping the nipple back in his mouth. Anne's whole body was trembling with need and remembered pleasure. She ran her fingers through his hair as she arched her body backwards, thrusting her tits forward.

Gabe pressed her back, running his hand up between her legs as he pushed the hem of her dress up out of the way. He could smell her arousal. She was ripe and ready for him. He parted her labia with his fingers and stroked her, making her groan and spread her legs further.

"Please, Sir."

"I thought you didn't beg," he teased.

"Only you. I only beg for you," she purred.

Gabe continued to stroke her as he unfastened his fly and let his hard cock come out to play. It had wanted back inside her since she'd sat in his lap at the Dark Garden. That was no surprise, his cock wanted her all the time. He lined the head up with her opening and then pressed in, watching and feeling her convulse in climax just from his possession. He pushed in deep, pulled back and then drove into her depths, hearing her gasp as he did so.

He began thrusting in and out, faster than he normally did, but then he didn't normally fuck her on his desk at work. He'd fucked her plenty of times on his desk at home, but he did try to be circumspect at the hotel. He angled his plunging so that he stroked her sweet spot. He began slamming into her, trying to get deeper each time. Anne brought her legs up so that she could lock her feet behind his back.

"Gabe," she cried softly as her body tightened and her pussy clamped down, spasming all along his length, milking his cock as he began to empty himself into her.

He felt their mutual orgasm wash over them and fill them each with a deep and abiding peace and joy. He loved her in a way he'd never thought possible and thanked God each and every day that she had found her way out of the Void and into his arms.

In his pocket, his mobile vibrated. The text read: We've assembled the other swords. Are you with us?

Savoy Hotel
 London, England
 Two Days Later

Guests were seated in the Gondoliers Room at the Savoy. Holmes and Watson stood on either side of the aisle. Rachel and Anne had been determined to have a double wedding as most of the people attending were friends of both couples. The room was a celebration of opulence and style that was Venice in the early years of the Twentieth Century. The walls had murals of the fabled Italian city and crystal chandeliers sparkled in the light. It was luxurious and elegant and befitted the style of a former Queen of England.

Gabe stood waiting for his bride-to-be with a profound sense of peace, joy and satisfaction. Anne Boleyn, who had been offered up to a dynastically hungry monarch, had settled in as a modern day woman. She was currently exploring what she wanted to do. Money was not an issue as the cache of coins and jewels her cousin Madge had hidden for her days before her death had given them a wealth Gabe had never thought possible.

The harp struck the first notes of Mendelssohn's Wedding March. He and Holmes glanced at each other and then looked up the aisle to their brides. Rachel had chosen a traditional, ivory-colored wedding dress with a long train, while Anne had opted for a more avant guard dress that she'd designed herself. It showed off every inch of her lush figure in shades of the sterling silver rose. Anne and Rachel both carried bouquets of roses. Anne's were ivory-colored while Rachel's were sterling silver.

Anne laughed, and suddenly Gabe was glad the tuxedo jacket he'd chosen was long enough to cover the front of his trousers. As usual, when parted from her even for several hours, just hearing her voice, especially her laugh, made his whole-body light up with arousal. No two ways about it, he was completely, madly and irrevocably in love with an older woman—one who was almost five centuries his senior.

The two-carat diamond ring in the halo setting set with amethysts matched the diamond and amethyst collar around her neck. He'd had to fight a Yeoman Warder and the Angel of Death to keep her, but he'd done it with the help of his friends.

As she walked toward him, Gabe realized that when most people talked about a romance and a love that passed the test of time and stood for all eternity, they were just talking. He was marrying a former Queen of England, a woman who had faced her own execution with dignity and had found her own way back to the land of the living. And now she was his, and they would face the rest of forever together.

Meanwhile back in their Soho flat, *Courechouse* rattled in its cradle.

Thank you for reading *Submission!* I've got some free bonus content for you! Sign up for my newsletter https://www.subscribepage.com/VIPlist22019. There is a special bonus scene, just for my subscribers. Signing up will also give you access to free books, plus let you hear about sales, exclusive previews and new releases first.

Want to learn about Roark and Sage? Holmes and Rachel? Read ADVANCE and NEGOTIA-TION respectively, available on all platforms and ADVANCE is free!

Also in the Masters of the Savoy series are CONTRACT coming January 6, 2022 and BOUND coming February 10, 2022.

. . .

Don't think you can wait to see what happens with Saoirse and Felix in CONTRACT? Turn the page for a First Look into CONTRACT.

If you enjoyed this book we would love if you left a review, they make a huge difference for indie authors.

As always, my thanks to all of you for reading my books.

Take care of yourselves and each other.

FIRST LOOK

Contract
Masters of the Savoy

Present Day
Savoy Hotel
London, England

Saoirse Madigan woke to the sound of the ocean and the smell of the sea. She shook her head, trying to dispel the last vestiges of what many would call a dream, but which she knew to be a vision from the past. She wasn't anywhere near the ocean. She was in London, at the Savoy, and later today two of her closest friends, Rachel Moriarty and Anne Hastings, were getting married to two of the most gorgeous men she'd ever seen—Michael Holmes and Gabriel Watson.

Long before Saoirse had known she was a witch, she knew she had the Gift—she could see and feel things others could not. One of the first had been the ghost of a young girl of maybe eight or nine years old, wearing a yellow dress from the Victorian era. Saoirse had been about the same age and many years later guessed that the child had chosen her because they were of a similar age.

For the longest time, the child would simply appear, holding her bonnet in her hand and staring at Saoirse. Saoirse tried speaking to her, but the child didn't respond. As Saoirse grew older and tried to approach the apparition, it would disappear. When she turned fifteen, the child appeared and then turned and walked away as it dissipated into nothing.

Saoirse hadn't seen the little girl for years until the first time she visited her friend Rachel Moriarty, soon to be Holmes, at the Savoy. The first time she'd used the elevator to go up, the little girl had appeared and at the fifth floor, the elevator had stopped briefly, and the child had walked through the closed doors before the car began to rise again and stopped at Rachel's floor.

Curious. She hadn't seen the little girl, whom she had christened Victoria, for many years. Once she had discovered she was a witch, she had tried summoning her, but the child had never answered. Saoirse had not thought to see her again until she had appeared on the elevator with her at the Savoy.

Who is she? Why is she at the Savoy? And what does she want with me?

Saoirse sat up in the bed, swinging her legs over the side and standing up. She glanced toward the window that looked over the Thames. Victoria was standing there, staring at her.

"Hello, Victoria. I haven't seen you in a long time. I'm sorry if that isn't your name, but I've never been able to find out who you are or were," said Saoirse gently.

"They're all here, you know," the little girl said, speaking for the first time in all of their encounters. Saoirse felt a shiver run up her spine.

"Who? Who are all here?"

"All the lost ones," the ghostly girl said. "We've been waiting. I told them some day you would come for us. Some day you would lead us to the Light."

Saoirse felt as though she'd been punched in the gut. Her recent involvement with Anne and her escape from the Void had left her in no doubt as to where it was 'they' wanted to go.

"I don't know how to help you," Saoirse said.

The little girl turned, cocked her head to the side and said in a sing-song voice:

"They did not search for those who died;
The chapel bell did not knell;
When the Irish witch can answer why,
Then our spirits will arise from Hell
And with the King of Kings we will abide."

Masters of the Savoy

Advance
Negotiation
Submission
Contract
Bound

ABOUT THE AUTHOR

Other books by Delta James: https://www. deltajames.com/

If you're looking for paranormal or contemporary erotic romance, you've found your new favorite author!

Alpha heroes find real love with feisty heroines in Delta James' sinfully sultry romances. Welcome to a world where true love conquers all and good triumphs over evil! Delta's stories are filled with erotic encounters of romance and discipline.

If you're on Facebook, please join my closed group, Delta's Wayward Pack! Don't miss out on the book discussions, giveaways, early teasers and hot men!

https://www.facebook.com/ groups/348982795738444

Ghost Cat Canyon

Determined - https://books2read.com/ghostcatdetermined

Untamed - https://books2read.com/ghostcatuntamed

Bold - https://books2read.com/ghostcatbold

Fearless - https://books2read.com/ghostcatfearless

Strong - https://books2read.com/ghostcatstrong

Boxset - https://books2read.com/Ghostcatset

Tangled Vines

Corked – https://books2read.com/corked1

Uncorked - https://books2read.com/uncorked

Decanted - https://books2read.com/decanted

Breathe - https://books2read.com/breathe1

Full Bodied - https://books2read.com/fullbodied

Late Harvest - https://books2read.com/lateharvest

Boxset 1 – https://books2read.com/TVbox1

Boxset 2 – https://books2read.com/Tvbox2

Mulled Wine – https://books2read.com/mulledwine

Wild Mustang

Hampton - https://books2read.com/hamptonw

Mac - https://books2read.com/macw

Croft – https://books2read.com/newcroft-dj

Noah - https://books2read.com/newnoah-dj

Thom - https://books2read.com/newthom-dj

Reid - https://books2read.com/newreid-dj

Wayward Mates

Brought to Heel: https://books2read.com/u/m0w9P7

Marked and Mated: https://books2read.com/u/4DRNpO

Mastering His Mate: https://books2read.com/u/bxaYE6

Taking His Mate: https://books2read.com/u/4joarZ

Claimed and Mated: https://books2read.com/u/bPxorY

Claimed and Mastered: https://books2read.com/u/3LRvM0

Hunted and Claimed: https://books2read.com/u/bPQZ6d

Captured and Claimed: https://books2read.com/u/4A5Jk0

Printed in Great Britain
by Amazon